52 Simple Ways to Talk with Your Kids About Faith

Opportunities for Catholic Families to Share God's Love

Jim Campbell

Introduction by
Tom McGrath, author of
Raising Faith-Filled Kids

LOYOLAPRESS.
CHICAGO

LOYOLAPRESS.

3441 N. ASHLAND AVENUE
CHICAGO, ILLINOIS 60657
(800) 621-1008
WWW.LOYOLABOOKS.ORG

Cover design: Beth Herman and Judine O'Shea
Interior design: Maggie Chung

Library of Congress Cataloging-in-Publication Data
Campbell, Jim, 1941-
    52 simple ways to talk with your kids about faith : opportunities for Catholic families to share God's love / Jim Campbell ; with Introduction by Tom McGrath.
     p. cm.
    Includes index.
    ISBN-13: 978-0-8294-2474-4
    ISBN-10: 0-8294-2474-1
    1. Family—Religious life. 2. Christian education of children. 3. Spiritual formation—Catholic Church. 4. Parent and child—Religious aspects—Catholic Church. I. Title. II. Title: Fifty two opportunities to talk with your kids about faith.
    BX2351.C26 2007
    249—dc22
                                       2007012321

Printed in the United States of America
08 09 10 11 12 Bang 10 9 8 7 6 5 4 3 2 1

For Elaine and Michele

Contents

Introduction by Tom McGrath

I'm really good at coming up with what-I-should've-saids. Those are the thoughtful, clever comments that occur to me after a conversation is over. Hours later, when I am replaying the scene in my mind, I can be fairly witty, persuasive, and insightful. But on the spot, I often let golden chances pass me by.

That's why I wish I'd had Jim Campbell's helpful book when my children were growing up. Like most parents I know, I longed to have meaningful conversations with my children about life's challenges and the value of faith in rising to meet them. Talking to our kids about things that matter is not always easy. I know that lecturing is futile, and yet not communicating our beliefs is clearly an abdication of our role as responsible, caring parents.

The best conversations I had with my children when they were growing up happened naturally, in the course of daily life—in the car, waiting for a bus, over grilled cheese sandwiches or meat loaf at our beat-up kitchen table. Often they happened when the kids would come home from basketball practice or from being out with friends and I'd notice that one of them was feeling particularly high or low, elated or disturbed. What I came to see was that I needed to become adept at using life's ordinary opportunities to weave conversations about values into daily life.

Jim Campbell's book is a great way to prepare and practice for those moments, and even to learn how to recognize them when they arise. What I appreciate about Jim is that he not only has a fine and creative grasp of theology, but he also has proven experience as an involved father, a doting grandfather, and a man of faith. He takes great care to practice what he preaches when it comes to engaging his children and grandchildren in lively conversations about faith.

Jim is never preachy; he models the utmost respect for the faith of everyone he encounters—no matter what age or state in life. He understands that he has a role to play in nurturing the faith of the young people in his care, yet he also honors and trusts each child's budding relationship with God. In this book, Jim freely gives the benefit of his theological scholarship and, more important, his wisdom as one who has faithfully walked the path before us.

Recent research shows that parents have far more influence than commonly suspected in the formation of their child's character and behavior—far more influence than peers, popular media, and the dubious role models that can chill a parent's heart. We have more effect on our child's moral development than we realize—or at least we can, if we choose to step into that role to the best of our ability. (Note: there's no such thing as "perfect" when it comes to being a parent.)

And the good news is that we are not alone in that challenge. Once we make the slightest move toward the goal of nurturing our child's life in faith, we can be sure the Holy Spirit will whoosh in to help and guide us. In fact, I've always found that the Holy Spirit is the one who does all the heavy lifting—if I will only accept the help.

Sometimes that help from the Holy Spirit comes in the form of an increased ability to simply listen to our children. As a parent, I've often been so eager to get my point across that I failed to first hear what one or the other of my daughters had to say. If I can actively listen, I will create a safe place for her to explore what she's feeling and what wisdom is available to her. When I manage to simply listen, I often discover that the message I was hoping to get across has already taken root in my child's heart and conscience.

Having meaningful conversations with your child also opens up the wonderful possibility of praying together. If your child talks about a difficult situation at school or with friends—or even if your child is troubled but doesn't feel like talking about it right now—you can gently introduce the idea of saying a quick prayer about the situation. "Can we pray about that together?" is an easy way to move from discussion to prayer. And you can model ways to turn life events over to the care of God: "Loving God, when I feel hurt by friends, I want to either run away or hurt them back. Help us to know your love for us, and feel it deep in our hearts, so that we might overcome our hurt and love others as you love us."

In the great musical *Les Misérables*, Jean Valjean takes the young child Cosette into his care. He is deeply moved by this sacred responsibility and promises Fantine, Cosette's dying mother, that he will care for the child in both body and soul. He sings, "I will raise her to the light." This is the challenge of everyone who cares for children—to raise them to the light. And while there may be grand moments along the way, most of that raising will be done in seemingly small moments, such as when we think to ask the right question and engage our children's hearts and minds and souls in conversation about life and faith. This book will help you do that. May God bless you on your way.

To the Parent:
How to Use 52 Simple Ways

This book is designed especially for parents who want to pass on a faith in God to their children but are unsure how to do this or are challenged to find a way that feels natural. The book is designed to show parents how to use ordinary situations and events to teach their children about faith. The fifty-two "simple ways," or lessons, are based upon the teachings of the Catholic Church. The author, Jim Campbell, is an accomplished theologian and catechist as well as a husband, a father of two, and a grandfather of six. He brings to these lessons a lifetime of study and experience.

The lessons can be used in a variety of ways. You can work through the book, beginning with lesson #1 and ending with #52. Or you can simply page through and find the lesson that best fits the child and the situation.

The four indexes in the back of the book can also help you locate the lesson that is most timely and appropriate. The **Topical Index of Natural Teachable Moments** lists the many situations that might apply to your child right now. The **Guide to Scripture Readings** focuses on the Bible stories and excerpts, providing the lesson numbers that correspond with them. The **Index of Faith Themes by Category** organizes the topics of faith and the lessons that go with them. There is also the **Index of Terms and Proper Names**. All of these indexes provide corresponding lesson numbers.

These lessons are meant to guide and support you, the parent. They begin by listing the faith themes covered by the lesson and the situations in which the lesson might be applied. A short reflection helps you focus on the themes for yourself. In the sidebar, "To Support You," a Scripture reference is provided, followed by "What the Church Says about This Topic."

When you are ready to approach your child, the "Starting the Conversation" segment offers a suggestion for doing so. Following that is helpful information for relating to children, such as "To Help You Listen," or "To Help You Connect."

Each lesson ends with an optional prayer that you and your child can pray together.

Please use the various components of these lessons in a way that suits your needs. These opportunities should be times of natural and unintimidating conversation. The goal is to create some space and time in which your child feels free to relate to you honestly about his or her faith life. Some conversations will be light and even humorous, while others will come with more difficulty and seriousness. Some of these lessons deal with painful or stressful situations, such as a death in the family, social injustices in the world, or a child's feeling that she will never fit in or have a friend. Other lessons invite you to involve other family members or people in the larger community.

Whatever your child is going through, God has wisdom, grace, and comfort to offer. And much of the time those gifts are delivered through a parent's love, attentiveness, and patience. Trust the Holy Spirit to be present as you seek to be present to your child. And don't be surprised if you learn a lot yourself! As you watch the spiritual growth in your child, you will see, more and more, how God is working in all the details of your life together.

1

Serving as your child's image of God

Faith Themes

God is loving Father to us, as taught by Jesus.
We are children of God and can therefore have an intimate father-child relationship with God.

Natural Teachable Moments

- On Father's Day, when family and community talk involves honoring fathers
- When watching a TV program or cartoon about families or father figures
- During ordinary family time, such as a meal, a weekend outing, or a game

WHAT A WONDERFUL FOSTER FATHER JOSEPH WAS TO JESUS. From the time Jesus was born, Joseph cared deeply for him—protecting, loving, and teaching him. In return, Jesus had the greatest respect for Joseph.

It can be overwhelming and a little frightening to know that we are our children's primary teachers in life. The family environment is the first place in which fundamental values form, and it's where children learn what it means to be a loving parent. What children learn in the home will heavily influence how they respond when they hear that Jesus tells us to refer to God as Father. What does your parenting teach your children about the meaning of "father"?

Starting the Conversation

Share with your child something you have learned from her. Ask her to identify what she has learned from you, your spouse, or other adults in, or especially close to, your family. This is a great opportunity to observe how your child interprets your words and actions.

To Help You Connect

Children love to hear about themselves, to know that they are important to their parents and that they have an effect on the lives of those they love. It's good to let your child know that you learn things from her. Don't be afraid to show her that you don't always have all the answers and that you, too, are learning. Explain that faith is a lifelong journey and that we never stop growing, at any age—and that's an exciting and wonderful thing.

TO SUPPORT YOU

SUGGESTED BIBLE READING
Jesus speaks of the relationship between himself and the Father and us:
John 14:23

WHAT THE CHURCH SAYS ABOUT THIS TOPIC
Jesus reveals to us that God is our loving Father. *Abba,* the term Jesus uses to address his Father in the New Testament, is a term of intimacy and closeness. It is similar to children calling their father "Dad." God gave us his Son, Jesus, to teach us that God is our Father. In Jesus we share this special closeness of intimate relationship with God. Therefore, all prayer is primarily addressed to God as Father.

A Prayer Moment with Your Child

Let's thank God for being our Father and for sending us his Son, Jesus:

Thank you, God, for being my Father,
who always loves me.
And thank you for giving us Jesus
to teach us about you.
Amen

2

Blessing your child

Faith Themes

The love of the Father, Son, and Holy Spirit is the source of all love.
We use the sign of the cross as a prayer of blessing.

Natural Teachable Moments

- Whenever you wish to bless your child, such as when he leaves on a school trip or for an overnight with a friend
- When your child sees you or someone else, such as a sports figure, make the sign of the cross
- When your child sees the pope or other church figure on TV blessing the crowds

A SIMPLE WAY WE IDENTIFY OURSELVES AS CHRISTIANS is by praying the **sign of the cross.** We open and close our personal prayer time with the sign of the cross, but we can use it especially as a sign of blessing for our children. A priest is not the only person who can bless someone; you can, too. You can give your children a blessing anytime you wish. This simple gesture speaks of a very deep bond that we have with our children, deeper even than our human relationship with them. In praying the sign of the cross over them or tracing it on their foreheads, we acknowledge that God is the source of all the blessings our children receive through us. We acknowledge the limits of what we can do and open ourselves to the limitless source of God's love for us. Love is the gift we have received in our children and the gift we return in blessing.

Starting the Conversation

Share with your child a memory of a time when you realized that God had blessed you. Then, if you wish, bless your child and explain what you are doing and why. Allow him to ask questions about the blessing.

To Help You Connect

If sharing your faith and other meaningful experiences with your child is a relatively new undertaking for you, spend a few moments each day to go through the following process: Reflect on your own faith experiences, beliefs, and questions—and how you might share those with your child one day if the opportunity should arise. Pray for the **Holy Spirit's** assistance in your efforts. Then, when a natural teachable moment arises, you will find that you're better prepared to respond to it and that the Holy Spirit will guide you or even speak through you.

TO SUPPORT YOU

SUGGESTED BIBLE READING
Through love, God lives in us and we live in God: 1 John 4:7–12

WHAT THE CHURCH SAYS ABOUT THIS TOPIC
God is the source of all love. God demonstrated his love in creation by sending his only son to save us. We love God in return by making his love visible in the world. When we love others and ourselves, we are bringing to life the love God has for all of us. What God asks of us is that we share with one another the same kind of loving-kindness that God shares with us.

One way we make God's love visible in the world is by blessing ourselves or others by praying the sign of the cross. The sign of the cross is an external expression of our relationship with God. It symbolizes God blessing us and also God's embracing us with blessings. At the same time, in the sign of the cross we express our belief in God, as the one from whom all our blessings come. The Israelites taught us to approach God always as one who blesses.

Christians follow this tradition of prayer, and in addition we praise God for giving us Jesus Christ. When we bless someone with the sign of the cross, we remember the **Trinity** of persons who bless us: Father, Son, and Holy Spirit. We especially recall the life, death, and resurrection of Jesus Christ. We trace the cross of Jesus upon a person or in the air above him. As we make the sign of the cross, we remember God's love, found in the past but also with us here and now. When we trace this holy sign above our children—or on their foreheads, hearts, or shoulders—we remember that they are blessed in mind and heart and all their being. As we do this, we pray aloud or silently: "In the name of the Father, and of the Son, and of the Holy Spirit. Amen."

A Prayer Moment with Your Child

Let's thank God for sending his only son to save us, and for all his blessings that surround us:

Loving God, thank you for sending Jesus to me
and for showing me how all good things come from you.
Help me bring your love with me everywhere I go.
In the name of the Father, the Son, and the Holy Spirit.
Amen

3

Relieving your child of too much pressure

Faith Themes

God wants our faith, not sacrifice.
Abraham's near sacrifice is a great lesson for us.

Natural Teachable Moments

- After your child brings home a noticeably good or bad report card
- While driving your child to or from an athletic or artistic practice
- When your child shows interest in a hobby or discipline

THE BIBLICAL STORY OF ABRAHAM'S WILLINGNESS TO SACRIFICE HIS SON ISAAC is a frightening one. How could God ask this of him? But the ultimate lesson of the story is that God did not want a child to be sacrificed. He stopped Abraham's sacrifice to show that the surrounding culture's practice of sacrificing children was wrong.

This Scripture story points to issues that we, as parents, can consider today. Although our culture does not condone the physical sacrifice of children, it does require more and more from them in order that they are seen as valuable in the world. What expectations do we have of our children? Do we insist on academic or athletic excellence beyond their capacity or interest? Do we insist that our way of doing things is the only way our children should follow? Are we frightened by the prospect of their wanting to follow vocations that we do not approve of? What help do we need from God to refrain from placing excessive demands on our children?

Starting the Conversation

Ask your child about her hopes and dreams for the future. Create an atmosphere in which you can listen without judging her choices or warning about how much study will be required to accomplish those goals.

To Help You Listen

When talking with your child about her hopes for the future, be sure to *listen* to her answer to the initial inquiry. Stop and consider it respectfully before responding. What was the emotion behind her response? Inspired hope? Confusion? Fear? Apathy? A desire to please you rather than to please herself? Reflect on this a moment and, in your response, remember how important it is to let your child know that you really heard her.

TO SUPPORT YOU

SUGGESTED BIBLE READING
Abraham is put to the test: Genesis 22:1–13

WHAT THE CHURCH SAYS ABOUT THIS TOPIC
God tests Abraham by telling him to offer Isaac in sacrifice. Abraham shows that he is willing to do anything for God. He prepares to perform the sacrifice, but at the last moment an angel stops him. The angel shows Abraham a ram caught in a bush, which Abraham offers as sacrifice.

The story of Abraham's willingness to sacrifice Isaac needs to be seen in the context of the times. People in the Canaanite cities surrounding the Israelite lands sacrificed their firstborn children to placate their gods. Abraham's story is an argument against the practice of child sacrifice.

A Prayer Moment with Your Child

We know how hard it can be to be trusting and faithful, so let's thank God for the examples of trust and faith he has given us:

God, thank you for the story of Abraham.
You keep your promises and do great things for us.
Help me always to trust in you.
Amen

4

Seeing beyond stereotypes

Faith Themes

Simeon in the Bible was able to recognize who Jesus was because he listened to the Holy Spirit.

We can, with the Spirit's help, learn to see people for who they are.

Natural Teachable Moments:

- When watching a movie or TV show that employs negative stereotypes
- When your child asks about a stereotype he has encountered
- After you, your child, or another family member has just made a judgment—or repeated someone else's judgment—based on a stereotype
- When preparing for a family trip to a place with foreign cultures and customs

WE ALL LIVE WITH STEREOTYPES. It's easy to make assumptions and to label people according to their looks, clothes, or ethnic origins. Take, for example, the story of **Joseph and Mary's** coming with the **baby Jesus** to the temple in observance of Jewish custom. Their humble offering of two turtledoves immediately labeled them as poor and unimportant, and this is how most people saw them. **Simeon,** however, inspired by the **Holy Spirit,** saw beneath the surface to recognize the promise of the Messiah in Jesus. The Holy Spirit calls us to see everyone though more pure eyes, the eyes of faith, and to discover how God cares for and loves each person. When you look at your child today, whom do you see? How can you nurture your child as the sacred person he is in God's eyes?

Starting the Conversation

Discuss a movie or TV show you have all seen in which a character starts out looking like a villain but is revealed to be a hero by the end of the story. Explore together what this can tell us about looking beyond first impressions.

To Help You Listen

You can learn a lot about your child's inner life by listening carefully to what qualities and characteristics made the character you are discussing together seem, in your child's perception, like a villain at first. Similarly, what qualities, characteristics, or values did the character exhibit by the story's end to change this perception in your child's eyes? Listen closely to discern the qualities or values that signify to your child "hero." Also, at what point in the story did his impression of the character change—and why? Hearing this can reveal a good deal about how your child is exercising his judgment.

TO SUPPORT YOU

SUGGESTED BIBLE READING
Simeon meets the holy family in the temple of Jerusalem: Luke 2:25–32

WHAT THE CHURCH SAYS ABOUT THIS TOPIC
In the biblical story of Simeon and the presentation of the baby Jesus at the temple, we see an example of how God helps us recognize what is really important in our relationships.

God promised Simeon, a righteous and devout man, that he would not die before seeing the Messiah he was waiting for. Many people at the time would have expected the Messiah—the prophesized savior of the Jewish people—to be born of a royal family or to come from among the important high priests.

One day an ordinary-looking couple with a child entered the temple in Jerusalem. They had come to present their son to God, bringing with them an offering of two turtledoves. Simeon, by now an old man with tired eyes, probably did not see Mary, Joseph, and the baby Jesus too clearly. He did, however, recognize that this seemingly unnoteworthy child was the Messiah. Through the Holy Spirit and with the eyes of faith, he saw beneath the surface and recognized in the infant God's promise fulfilled.

The teaching of the church stresses the importance of listening to and recognizing the work of the Holy Spirit in all our relationships. The same Spirit who came to Mary, Joseph, and Simeon is with us today and is helping us recognize God's presence in our own lives. By listening to the Holy Spirit we learn how to see more truly and to care for others and for ourselves.

A Prayer Moment with Your Child

The Holy Spirit has a special place in our lives, as our guide and helper. Let's invite the Holy Spirit to show us the way today and everyday:

Holy Spirit, thank you for being my guide.
Help me to always listen carefully to you
and to do what you guide me to do.
Amen

5

Facing new and uncertain situations

Faith Themes

Mary said yes to God in faith and trust, and she became the mother of Jesus. Mary loves and prays for us.

Natural Teachable Moments

- On your child's first day of school or with a new club or team
- When your family is about to have an addition, young or old
- Before a May crowning ritual or anytime in May, Mary's month

SCHOLARS TELL US THAT AT THE TIME OF THE ANNUNCIATION—when the archangel Gabriel announced to **Mary** that she had been chosen to bear a son, called Jesus, who would be the Son of God—Mary was probably in her mid-teens. This was the normal age for a girl to be betrothed in marriage. Mary was at the time betrothed to **Joseph.** She was from an otherwise undistinguished family, living in an occupied country. It is no wonder Mary questioned God's plan for her; nevertheless, she believed God's message and faced the future confident that God would be with her.

We face an unknown future. As we get older and move through life, we discover that things are not as certain as they might have seemed once. We cannot help but wonder about the world in which we are bringing up our children. Mary faced all these issues with faith and hope. Mary loves and prays for us now. Never be afraid to ask for her help.

Starting the Conversation

Although your child may be quite young, she still has to make decisions. Ask her about some of the decisions she had to make today. After listening to her response, ask how and why she decided on each particular choice, if she hasn't described this already. Reflect on your child's response, as this is a great opportunity to observe her decision-making process. Explain to her how present decisions often affect the future.

To Help You Pray

Prayer gives your child an opportunity to speak with and listen to God. Sometimes we pray together by speaking out loud or singing. Sometimes we pray silently in our hearts and minds, using our own words. Sometimes we pray without using words—either just listening silently to God or simply sharing our presence with God and reflecting upon God's presence with us. In a world so filled with noise, your child may have little experience with silence. Talk with her about the value of these prayer-filled moments and encourage her to explore times in her days when she could be silent and be with God.

TO SUPPORT YOU

SUGGESTED BIBLE READING

Jesus' birth is announced to Mary, who in a spirit of humility praises God for choosing her: Luke 1:26–38 and 46–50

What the Church Says about This Topic

Our Catholic faith teaches us that Mary was a virgin her entire life, both before and after the birth of Jesus. Virgins were often looked down on in the Jewish society at that time. The birth of the Savior to a virgin living in an obscure village was a powerful sign of God's special love for the lowly people of the world.

It is important to understand that when Mary was asked to be the mother of the Savior, she was completely free to accept or reject the offer. Her response, "Let it be done to me," was a great act of faith. Because she did not understand all of what was happening, she must have known that there would be difficulties ahead.

Because she replied yes to the angel's announcement and agreed to become the mother of Jesus, the church has declared Mary to be the **mother of God.** Because she was the first to say yes to the Messiah, the church has declared her to be both a saint and the mother of the church.

Mary is very special to Catholics. We feel close to her because of her role in salvation history and because of her closeness to Jesus. Catholics believe Mary loves and prays for us. We do not worship Mary; we venerate her because we know that she intercedes for us to God.

A Prayer Moment with Your Child

Let's ask Jesus to help us trust God as Mary did:
Jesus, there are many uncertain things about life.
Help me to trust God and say yes to God's will,
as Mary did.
Amen

6

Setting priorities

Faith Themes

Our life priorities are moral choices.
God wants us to respect others and live in peace.

Natural Teachable Moments

- When you first suggest that you and your child try praying together, if you do not already have regular prayer time
- When your family is planning where and how you will celebrate religious holidays, such as Easter and Christmas
- During times of difficulty or when big decisions must be made, when the family comes together in prayer or discussion

FRANCIS BORGIA (1510–1572) WAS A RICH NOBLEMAN IN SPAIN. He was born into an extremely wealthy and influential Spanish family, and he enjoyed being a person of wealth and high social standing. He married when he was nineteen, rubbed elbows with royalty, and had at his disposal nearly everything he desired. Then one day a close friend, the Empress Isabella, died, and Francis realized that his wealth would not last forever or buy him happiness. Her death showed him that earthly possessions and social status are fleeting. Then Francis's wife died, which convinced Francis to give up his many possessions and join the Society of Jesus, commonly known as the Jesuits. Francis became a Jesuit priest, founded a Jesuit college, and was eventually made the head of the order. No longer focused on money and material possessions, Francis had shifted his attention toward serving God. His tireless devotion to Jesus Christ and to the order led many to see him as the order's second founder. He was made a saint in 1671.

Like Francis, we make decisions every day that teach our children where our priorities lie. They can see how important God is in our lives. If your child made a list today of what your family's priorities are, where would God rank?

Starting the Conversation

Share with your child the role God has played in your upbringing, your relationship with your spouse, or your family life. Ask your child what, other than perhaps attending **Mass,** shows him that God is a priority in your home. Invite him to make God a priority in his life, and if he agrees, brainstorm together about how you can demonstrate this as a family.

To Help You Listen

When asking your child for his perceptions of whether God is a priority in your family's life, listen closely to his response and accept it for what it is. If he is less aware of God's priority in your home than you feel is the case, resist any urge to correct his answer by insisting upon what he should have seen, heard, or felt. You may express your priorities, or even point out evidence to the contrary that he hasn't noticed for himself, but remember that his perceptions are real and valid. It's good practice to acknowledge this. What you *intended* to communicate about the family's priorities is not as important as what your child is actually *perceiving.* Ultimately you want your intended communication and the child's perceptions to align, but if they do not, you can accept this as valuable feedback.

Your child may have perceived that God is more important in your family life than you would have answered. If this is the case, perhaps there is more going on under the surface than you are aware of, and you need to take a closer look at God's presence in your daily life. Whatever the answer, carefully listening to your child's response is an opportunity for learning about his inner life. Remember, having meaningful conversation with your child means that *you* learn and grow as well.

TO SUPPORT YOU

SUGGESTED BIBLE READING

The early Christian community is urged to turn from evil and do good:
1 Peter 3:8–12

WHAT THE CHURCH SAYS ABOUT THIS TOPIC

The priorities we set reveal what is important to us. Our life priorities are moral choices; they will affect not only the decisions we make but also the lives of those around us.

The well-being of the community is at stake when we make choices. We must consider how those choices will affect individuals and the community (such as the family, the neighborhood, and the parish). When we make good moral choices, we show respect for God and others, and we cultivate peace.

A Prayer Moment with Your Child

It can be hard in our busy lives to keep God at the center, so let's thank God for the examples of commitment and faith he has given us in the saints. And let's ask for God's help to love God as the saints did:

God, thank you for St. Francis Borgia and for all the saints.
Their dedication and trust in you is an inspiration.
Help me to make you a priority in my life,
today and every day.
Amen

7

Knowing the true self as a good creation

Faith Themes

The human family is created in the image and likeness of God.
God created everything good, and there are good aspects of things we usually think of as bad.

Natural Teachable Moments

- When your child wonders how she, or the world, began
- When your child worries about "bad" people or questions the nature of things
- After your child uses the slang expression, "'s all good."

WE ARE FASCINATED BY THE STORY OF HOW THINGS BEGAN. Our children are fascinated by stories of how they were born: who was present, what time it happened, how exciting it was. We have that same sense of wonder about the beginning of the world. The story of how the world began is told in the first chapter of Genesis; in fact, the word "genesis" means "in the beginning." The story was written when the Jewish people were in exile in Babylon between 597 and 537 BC. They wrote the story because their children in Babylonian schools were learning the Babylonian story of creation that was filled with bloody battles. The Babylonians taught that the human family was created from the blood of an evil god. The Jewish writer of Genesis wanted to make it clear that the world was, and continues to be, created by God and that God's creation is good. Celebrate God's good world today.

Starting the Conversation

Remind your child that the Bible says, and the Catholic faith teaches, that from the beginning God created everything good. Then ask your child if she really believes that everything was created good. Ask her if she believes she was created good.

To Help You Ask Questions

You may choose to be lighthearted with this question at first, but then ask your child in a manner that shows her you are being serious. For example: "No, really—do you truly believe it?" If she has doubts or does not believe in the original goodness of creation, resist any urge to try to force her to believe. Share with her what *you* believe and why. Be careful to let her know that this "goodness" the Bible is talking about is not a behavior or a set of rules to follow; that would be goodness that earns God's favor. The goodness talked about in Genesis is the true nature of people, placed there by God. Our natural goodness is a reflection of God's nature; it is what Scripture means when it says we are made in God's image.

TO SUPPORT YOU

SUGGESTED BIBLE READING

God creates the world and people: Genesis 1:1–2:4 and 2:4–25

WHAT THE CHURCH SAYS ABOUT THIS TOPIC

There are two distinct **stories of creation.** The first, in Genesis 1:1–2:4, was written during the Babylonian exile (587–537 BC). The authors wrote this story to counteract the influence of the Babylonian culture, more specifically its violent creation story. The first chapter of Genesis shows how God calmly created the heavens and the earth and how he upholds them daily, having declared everything to be good.

The second creation account, Genesis 2:4–25, relates a story of creation that was written earlier, probably during the reigns of David and Solomon, between 1005 and 928 BC. This earlier version emphasizes that the human race was created by God to cooperate with him in caring for the earth. It also emphasizes the fundamental equality of men and women.

Human beings have been created in the image of God. This means that we are equal to one another and are God's representatives; our behavior toward the world, its living beings, and its resources should reflect how God would act. Human dominion over the created world is supposed to reflect God's dominion over all things. And God's dominion is based on our care for the world God created.

A Prayer Moment with Your Child

Let's thank God for his creation and for helping us treat it as he would:

God, thank you for making the earth a good place
and for creating people to be good.
Help me act in ways that show people
I am made in your image.
Amen

8

Facing moral choices

Faith Themes

God gives us the freedom to make our own choices.
Moral choices affect our relationships with God and other people; moral decisions have moral consequences.

Natural Teachable Moments

- When your child is being willful and threatens you with bad behavior
- When your child is reluctant to act on your authority alone or challenges the authority of an adult who responds, "Because I told you to."
- After you, your child, or another family member has made a decision that results in clearly observable consequences

[Note: this Biblical story is recommended for slightly older adolescents.]
SOMETIMES WE DON'T KNOW WHAT TO MAKE OF THE OLD TESTAMENT. It contains so many violent stories of war and betrayal. For example, the story of **King David and Bathsheba** could appear in today's tabloids. David had a moral choice to make, and he made the wrong one. He abused the freedom he had as king when he took Uriah's wife and then had Uriah killed. The prophet Nathan called David back to his senses and to repentance. David was sorry, and he did repent, and God forgave him—but David still had to live with the

consequences of his decision for the rest of his life. David raised a family and it was beset with division and conflict.

Unfortunately, like David, we can be tempted to interpret our freedom of choice as a right to do whatever we want. Our children are especially susceptible to this temptation because they are learning to make choices on their own. God reminds us that choice is not just a gift granted to human beings; it is a responsibility as well. How you use this gift will affect your life and your relationships with God and others. Christians can find true freedom only as they follow the ways of Christ. Christian freedom is not acted out in selfish ways but in service to others.

Starting the Conversation

Have a discussion about what freedom means to you and to your child. Share one way you would like to be freer, and ask your child how he would like to be free. Lead the conversation to the relationship between freedom and the necessity on everyone's part to act in a responsible way because, though we are free to act as we want, our actions naturally have consequences we must live with.

To Help You Listen

When your child is thinking about how to answer a question, remain quiet and let him process his thoughts and feelings. Be patient and resist the need to prompt him. Just wait. Often, a child feels more encouraged to talk when the parent remains silent but expectant after asking a question.

TO SUPPORT YOU

SUGGESTED BIBLE READING

Two stories show us two moral choices: Ruth 1–4 and 2 Samuel 11:1–17

WHAT THE CHURCH SAYS ABOUT THIS TOPIC

The Catholic Church teaches that God's grace is necessary for salvation but that people are free to respond positively or negatively to God's grace. In the sixteenth century, the Council of Trent made the doctrine of **free will** an official teaching of the Catholic faith. This doctrine holds that people can choose among different courses of action and that this freedom to choose also makes us morally responsible for what we do.

Catholic morality accepts the possibility that people can be limited by factors such as fear, ignorance, passion, and habits, but the church insists that the human person is fundamentally free and can be held responsible for his or her actions.

When we make a morally wrong decision, God's forgiveness is available to us. We will always receive that forgiveness when we show openness to it through our repentance and a desire to change. We must keep in mind, however, that the bad choices we make bring bad consequences that are not automatically wiped out by repentance and forgiveness. One of the ways we learn to trust God and to make better choices is by accepting the responsibility for the harmful consequences of the bad choices we have made.

A Prayer Moment with Your Child

Let's thank God for guiding us through the example of others, such as the stories of people in the Bible:

Thank you, God, for giving us examples in the Scriptures
of both good and bad choices.
Help me learn from those stories
to avoid making bad choices myself.
Amen

9

Embracing change

Faith Themes

The Holy Spirit is like the wind, which blows where it wills.
We grow in the gifts of the Holy Spirit.

Natural Teachable Moments

- As the family is preparing to relocate or when a good friend moves away
- When your child's summer plans fall through or she must attend summer school or another academic program
- When your family makes a household change, such as tightening the budget or putting limits on TV watching and Internet surfing

WE SEE CHANGE GOING ON EVERY DAY. The child who comes home from school is different from the child you sent to school. Each day life becomes more complex. We can easily become nostalgic for a time when things were simpler, when our child's problems could be settled with a hug and a few comforting words. But nothing remains static. As change happens—and it will—we have God's promise that the **Holy Spirit** will be with us, guiding and upholding us. Jesus compares the presence of the Holy Spirit with the wind that blows where it will. We don't know where it comes from or where it is going. The image is one of mystery, movement, and change.

Starting the Conversation

Sometimes we can make change happen. Ask your child together with other family members what changes for the better they would like to make as a family.

To Help You Pray

The Holy Spirit is the fundamental intercessor, leader, and guide during all prayer. Learn to respect your child's spirituality; when your child is in prayer, remember that her reflections in prayer are hers alone. You show respect for your child's conversation with God by letting her keep these thoughts and feelings to herself. You may let your child know she can share with you her prayerful reflections if she'd like—you will certainly welcome hearing them—but this is not necessary. She is free to keep these conversations of the heart between herself and God. Prayer is a very personal and intimate experience.

TO SUPPORT YOU

SUGGESTED BIBLE READING

The work of the Spirit is like a wind that blows where it chooses: John 3:8

WHAT THE CHURCH SAYS ABOUT THIS TOPIC

There are several titles for the Holy Spirit in Scripture. Jesus called the Spirit the "Paraclete" (which means "he who is called to one's side," or "consoler" or "comforter"), as well as the Spirit of Truth. St. Paul used the following titles: the Spirit of Promise, the Spirit of Adoption (referring to us as adopted children of God), the Spirit of the Lord, and the Spirit of God.

In the Old Testament's book of Isaiah 11:2–3, the **gifts of the Holy Spirit** are described. These gifts are a permanent willingness—given to us by the Holy Spirit—that makes it possible for us to do what God asks of us. In this passage, the gifts are considered ones that the prophesized Messiah would possess. Through Jesus, we also receive these six gifts in the **sacrament of confirmation.**

Wisdom helps us recognize the importance of others and the importance of keeping God central in our lives. **Understanding** is the ability to comprehend the meaning of God's message. **Knowledge** is the ability to think about and explore God's revelation, and to recognize that there are mysteries of faith beyond our understanding. **Counsel** is the ability to see the best way to follow God's plan when we have choices that relate to it. **Fortitude** is the courage to do what we know is right. **Piety** is a spiritual gift that helps us pray to God in true devotion. And **fear of the Lord** is the feeling of amazement before God, who is all present, and whose friendship we do not want to lose.

A Prayer Moment with Your Child

With the Holy Spirit's help, let's quiet ourselves and meet God in our hearts:

Holy Spirit, thank you for helping me pray
and for filling me with the grace I need
to grow in my relationship with God.
Help me be a living sign of Jesus' presence in the world.
Amen

10

Developing childhood heroes

Faith Themes

Our heroes help form our conscience.

Free will leads to moral responsibility.

Natural Teachable Moments

- As your child plans to go to a sports event, concert, or convention featuring one of his pop idols
- When you and your child watch a movie, TV show, or news program featuring someone's heroic deeds
- When your child sees firefighters, police officers, soldiers, or any public servant on TV, in malls, in parades, or on the street

WHO WERE YOUR CHILDHOOD HEROES WHEN YOU WERE GROWING UP? Think for a moment about when you were your child's age and what you wanted to be. Who were your heroes when you were fifteen? Twenty? Which people were the most influential in shaping your future? It's important to think about these people because they helped you form your ideas about right and wrong. As a parent, you are now a living example of what it means to live in relationship with God and others. How are you influencing the formation of your child's conscience?

Starting the Conversation

Ask your child who his heroes are and why. As he answers, consider what these choices say about him.

To Help You Connect

Children love the idea that their parents once were small and looked up to others. They love hearing stories about their parents' childhood heroes. Talk to your child about the person or persons who inspired you when you were his age. Try to paint a picture in his mind of the person and his or her relationship to you. Explain some of the differences between heroes during your childhood and your heroes today. For example, if your childhood hero was a celebrity or sports star, you might explain that there was no Internet back then and you couldn't read stories about public personalities on their fan websites; explain what you did instead. But most important, express what values and virtues this person represented to you that you found so attractive. If you no longer find these values attractive in a person, explain why. It's important that your child learn that our values can change as we grow older and wiser. If you still find these values attractive, point out someone your child knows who exhibits these values today, like a family member—or perhaps the child himself.

TO SUPPORT YOU

SUGGESTED BIBLE READING

Moses urges the Israelites to take the **Ten Commandments** to heart and to teach their children: Deuteronomy 6:4–9

WHAT THE CHURCH SAYS ABOUT THIS TOPIC

An **examination of conscience** is a prayerful review of how we have been living in light of what the Gospel asks of us. It is often based on a reflection on each of the Ten Commandments and an assessment of how you have or have not been faithful to that commandment since your last examination. It can also be based on the virtues, such as justice, **fortitude,** and temperance, since they are the habits we develop in order to lead moral lives. A true examination of conscience is more than a prayerful consideration of one's past. Its major focus should be on the future and the continual conversion to the life of discipleship.

It is not always easy to make the right choices, but we have a soul and the **free will** to choose to do good. **Original sin** does not destroy free will. In fact, if we did not have free will, we would not be morally responsible for the consequences of our choices. However, our free will depends on an informed conscience. Our responsibility for our actions can be reduced, harmed, or negated by a conscience that is poorly formed because of ignorance, emotional illness or duress, various psychological or social factors, or bad examples given by others. At the same time, this does not mean that such ignorance and errors are free of moral responsibility. We must always obey our conscience and work to have it well informed and corrected of any errors.

A Prayer Moment with Your Child

Let's spend a few moments with God, and ask that God's love fill us:
Loving God, I see the world your great love has created.
Thank you for the people I can look up to in my life;
their choices and actions reflect your love.
Let your love fill me even more.
Amen

11

Seeing God's love and care for all people

Faith Themes

God created us because God loves us.
God gives us what we need and only wants the best for us.

Natural Teachable Moments:

- When your child is admiring the natural wonders of our world
- At a holiday meal, a party, or a feast, when good food and good company are plentiful
- When your child is feeling unsure about whether God loves her

WHEN YOU WALK INTO YOUR CHILD'S BEDROOM, WHAT DO YOU SEE? What is it that makes the room unique? Perhaps you see the quilt that was specially made by Grandma. Maybe pictures of sports or cartoon heroes adorn a wall. Books on dinosaurs or other favorite animals may fill bookcases. Drawings of dragons or butterflies may decorate the room. Think for a moment about how much you can learn about your child simply by noticing the things she loves and collects. In much the same way, we receive a reflection of who God is through the things present in his world. When we look thoughtfully at the world God created, and when we note the good things with which he surrounds us, we truly discover God's love and care for us.

Starting the Conversation

Talk with your child about something you saw today that reminded you of God. Then ask her to share any impression of things she saw that reminded her of God. Point out how these things demonstrate God's love for us.

To Help You Connect

When you feel that a meaningful conversation with your child has come to a close, allow for some transition time before launching into the next subject or activity. Take this time to reflect not only on your child's communication and behavior but on yourself as well: How do you feel right now? What were the movements of the Spirit within you as you were listening to your child and sharing with her? How might you have responded differently if you were to have this experience again?

TO SUPPORT YOU

SUGGESTED BIBLE READING

God provides food for the man and woman he created: Genesis 1:29

WHAT THE CHURCH SAYS ABOUT THIS TOPIC

The end of chapter 1 in Genesis teaches us about God's concern for the human family, represented by the first parents, **Adam and Eve.** God had placed Adam and Eve in a garden. In the Bible, the image of the garden, with its generous space set apart for the cultivation of plants, is an image of abundance, beauty, and the satisfaction of human need. The garden shows us a place of protection and seclusion, where human life can flourish. God intended for the needs of everyone to be met.

The images in this reading of Genesis help to counteract one of the more unfortunate ideas society seems to hold about God: that God is distant from us. We hear about God observing us from a distance. We may think that daily life is something we have to work out for ourselves. Genesis, however, reminds us that God created the world just for us, and that God calls us to grow in relationship with him and with one another.

We thank God for such a precious gift by acknowledging what a truly wonderful blessing it is. We do not take God's gift for granted, nor do we keep this beauty to ourselves. We thank God for what we received and remain grateful when we share it with others.

A Prayer Moment with Your Child

Let's thank God for creating and loving each one of us:

God, our Creator,
thank you for loving me and caring for me.
Amen

12

Describing family and faith identity

Faith Themes

Through the Holy Spirit, Christ unifies us and makes us holy.
The marks of Christ's church are one, holy, catholic, and apostolic.

Natural Teachable Moments

- Before a family reunion, or when visiting grandparents or attending a get-together with extended family
- When celebrating a family tradition that your child loves
- When looking at our country's flag or that of another country

MANY FAMILIES HAVE PARTICULAR WAYS TO IDENTIFY THEMSELVES. For example, in Europe there is a rich tradition of crests, shields, and flags that carry a family's identifying symbols. In the Celtic world, colorful tartans identify traditional family names. In Latin American culture, the icon that unifies people and gives them a common identity is **Our Lady of Guadalupe.** Although she appeared in what is now the outskirts of Mexico City, she belongs not only to the Mexican people but to the entire hemisphere. Besides the Virgin of Guadalupe, Latin American people identify themselves by their respective flags and anthems.

The Catholic Church has ways to identify itself, too. Its particular characteristics are **one, holy, catholic,** and **apostolic.** These four marks of the church are not characteristics that the church creates or develops or learns; they are qualities that Jesus Christ shares with his church through the **Holy Spirit.** Jesus is the source of unity and holiness. The Catholic Church is one because of Jesus, who is its head and whose Spirit unites different people and a diversity of gifts into one body. The church is holy because of Jesus; as the church lives in union with Christ, the Holy Spirit sanctifies and guides its actions. The church is catholic (the word means "all embracing") because its mission is to proclaim Christ to the whole world and to serve all people. And the church is apostolic because it remains faithful to the faith it received from the apostles.

How can your child see the holiness and faithfulness of the church? By the way members of the church love one another and make sacrifices to help other people in the world. Were people to look at your family as representative of the Catholic faith, what would they recognize in the way you speak, act, or relate to others? What identifying marks would they see in your family?

Starting the Conversation

Talk about any crest, symbol, traditional celebration, ritual, sign, or fabric pattern that identifies your family as coming from a particular heritage or tradition. Share its history with your child and explain why it is meaningful to you. Then brainstorm together about what your family would put on a new crest or a family website that would show the world what you value.

To Help You Pray

Begin prayer with your child by inviting him to still his heart and mind so as to focus quietly on God's presence. After praying, give him a few moments to pray silently to God in his own words. You might say something like: "Now, if you want, take a few moments to say to God whatever you'd like. You can pray this silently in your heart—and I'll be doing the same."

TO SUPPORT YOU

SUGGESTED BIBLE READING
The church has holy characteristics: Ephesians 4:1–6 and 15–16

WHAT THE CHURCH SAYS ABOUT THIS TOPIC
Catholics describe the church as "one, holy, catholic and apostolic" in the **Nicene Creed,** which we pray every Sunday during **Mass**. The Nicene Creed was written centuries ago to help Christians remember the important beliefs of the faith. The word *creed* means a statement of beliefs. The Nicene Creed is based on the creed developed at the Council of Nicea in AD 325. At this council, the bishops struggled to define how Jesus was equal in status to the Father while at the same time being the Son of the Father. The creed was given its final form in 381 by the bishops at the Council of Constantinople. In this revision, they expanded the language about the Holy Spirit. This is the creed held by all Christians, East and West, except for some Protestant churches that do not want to be based on a creed. In the relationship between the members of the **Trinity**, we can see, in the unity of the divine persons, a reflection of the unity we should have with one another.

A Prayer Moment with Your Child
Let's thank Jesus for the gift of his church:
Loving Jesus, thank you for creating a church
that shares in your holiness and love.
Help me to love the church
and to identify with unity and holiness, as it does.
Amen

13

Going through
life transitions

Faith Themes

We can have new life in God.
The sacraments of initiation help us with transition.

Natural Teachable Moments

- When you or your spouse is going back to work after being an at-home parent
- When your family loses or gains a member in your home—whether young or old, human or animal
- When an older sibling goes off to college or moves away from home

FROM THE WINDOW OF THEIR HOME, THE MOTHER AND HER CHILDREN could see a pair of birds building a new nest. As time passed, they could see tiny eggs in the nest and the careful way they were kept warm. They noticed how the birds chirped in warning if an animal or person came too close. Then tiny birds came out of their shells. As spring turned into summer, the tiny birds grew and learned how to fly. One day they were gone, leaving behind the empty nest.

Nature provides many examples of life's transitions. Most transitions in our lives are also spiritual transitions. These changes, though they may seem challenging as we face them, enable the birth of something new. As Christians, we celebrate these transitions in the **sacraments.** Through the sacraments we receive God's grace, and in the case of three sacraments—**baptism, confirmation,** and **Eucharist**—we receive new life in God.

Starting the Conversation

What significant transitions or changes is your family facing? Ask your child how she feels about the current or impending change. Explain that change is a natural part of life and that each transition is an opportunity for renewal and rebirth. Tell your child about the sacraments of the church, which provide the grace to help your family cope with these changes.

To Help You Connect

If you feel that a particular conversation with your child did not go well, be cautious of any desire to redo the conversation immediately. Often it's best to regroup and address the matter at another time. Take some time to replay the entire interchange and reflect on your feelings.

At what point did you feel out of harmony with your child?

- Right from the start? Perhaps you need to more carefully observe her moods and evaluate her readiness.
- After your child's comments? Perhaps your own expectations were impeding your ability to listen.
- When you didn't know how to answer your child's questions? Remember that a perfectly acceptable answer is, "I don't know; I'm still learning, too, but I'll look into that and tell you what I think later." And don't be afraid to broach the subject again at a more desirable time or to apologize to your child, if an apology is appropriate.

TO SUPPORT YOU

Suggested Bible Reading

Peter speaks of baptism in Spirit and following Jesus: Acts 2:38

What the Church Says about This Topic

The **sacraments of initiation** make us members of the Catholic Church. This membership entitles us to new life in Christ and fellowship with a Spirit-filled community.

Baptism is the sacrament of initiation by which we are introduced into the community of believers. Baptism removes **original sin** and incorporates us into Christ: it is a beginning, the start of life as a new creation, the beginning of a journey in following the footsteps of Jesus Christ.

Confirmation is the sacrament by which we are introduced into a fuller life in the **Holy Spirit.** The initiation involved in confirmation seals us in the Holy Spirit and incorporates us more fully into Christ. Confirmation is a beginning, the start of a life of service, the beginning of a life of dedicated work for the coming of God's kingdom.

Eucharist is the sacrament of initiation by which the incorporation into the Church begun in baptism and confirmation is brought to completion. In the Eucharist, Christ becomes food for our journey. The Eucharist always represents a new beginning, the constant renewal of the life of Christ within us.

A Prayer Moment with Your Child

Let's spend some time talking with and listening to God, and let's thank God for his gifts of grace:

Thank you, God, for your gift of grace,
which renews my life.
Help me to always stay close to you.
Amen

14

Making friends and being a friend

Faith Themes

We all need companions on our faith journey.

Jesus gives us the church as our community of spiritual friends and companions so that we can help one another and serve God's kingdom.

Natural Teachable Moments

- A couple of weeks after your child's first day of school or after joining a new club or sports team
- When you see your child playing with a new friend in the schoolyard, playground, or neighborhood
- Before you spend a few hours away from home while someone else stays with your child

EACH TIME OUR CHILDREN LEAVE OUR HOMES, they enter into the world at large. Along the way, they make new friends, some of whom become lifelong companions. Jesus knew the importance of having companions. In choosing Peter and the other apostles and disciples, he was taking the first step in establishing the church. In the church and especially in our parishes, companions in faith are waiting to walk with our children on their journeys toward God. Children's greatest influences are their parents. It is through the relationships children form within the family that they learn how to maintain relationships outside the family. By preparing your child now to make friends and to be a friend, you are giving him a priceless skill he will use throughout life.

Starting the Conversation

Jesus chose his companions carefully. Ask your child who his special friends are. What makes them such good friends? What does he learn from them? How does what he learns help him to follow Jesus? Perhaps you can tell him about one of your good friends and how that person has influenced the way you live.

To Help You Ask Questions

If your child puts off your question, defers, or simply answers, "I don't know," ask the question again, in an encouraging tone. Then pause and allow your silence to indicate that you are listening and awaiting a deeper response. Try to be attentive, however, to your child's state of mind, and don't force him to talk to you if he's not ready. If your child is very resistant to talking to you at a given moment, tell him that he doesn't have to answer now but maybe you will talk about this again sometime later. Try again—and again and again and again—at different times. A parent's persistence will eventually reap rewards.

TO SUPPORT YOU

SUGGESTED BIBLE READING

Jesus tells us we are friends when we follow him and do God's will: John 15:14

WHAT THE CHURCH SAYS ABOUT THIS TOPIC

There are several different ways of talking about the church. When we talk about the church as an institution, we stress those aspects of the church that enable it to function effectively to do God's will. The institutional church is a hierarchy: the pope is at its head, followed by organizational elements, such as dioceses and parishes. When we speak of the church as servant, we have in mind the social and charitable services the church provides, such as caring for the elderly and educating the young.

When we speak of the church as herald, we focus on the church's mission to proclaim the Good News to all nations. When we speak of the church as **sacrament,** we focus on the church as a sign and witness of Jesus' presence in the world and of the salvation he brings. And when we speak of the church as communion, we focus on a community of today's disciples providing friendship, help, and encouragement to one another as they journey together on the road to the kingdom. The church is our home, a faith-filled family given to us by God so that we will have companionship and support as we follow in the footsteps of Jesus.

A Prayer Moment with Your Child

Let's pray together and ask Jesus to help us be a good friend:
Thank you, loving Jesus, for showing me how to be a good friend.
You are a wonderful example for us to follow.
Help me to be kind and caring toward others,
the way you are.
Amen

15

Taking advantage of ordinary family time

Faith Themes

The family's love for one another is a reflection of the enduring love between Christ and his people.

The family is also known as the "domestic church."

Natural Teachable Moments:

- During family meals or when planning for the upcoming weekend
- While driving your child to and from activities
- When tucking your child into bed at night

CHILDREN CAN ASK WHAT SEEM LIKE IMPOSSIBLE QUESTIONS. One of these is, "What is God like?" All sorts of abstract answers come to mind. Terms such as *all powerful* and *almighty* swirl in our heads. The Christian answer can be found by looking to Jesus Christ. He is the one who came to tell us and show us what God is like. God is our loving Father. Jesus shows us how to love. Our children are receiving their fundamental understanding of what God is like from the way we relate to them. From us they are learning how a loving parent acts. From us they are learning the dignity of being a brother or sister in Jesus. And from us they are learning what it means to be a caring family.

Starting the Conversation

Share with your child what spending time with her and the whole family means to you. Recall a specific occasion or activity when having your family with you was especially meaningful to you. Ask your child what she would like to do this week for family time. You might share a bag of popcorn and a rental movie, play a board game, take a walk, or have ice cream cones in everyone's favorite flavor. Plan a special event when the family can be together without the usual distractions.

To Help You Connect

Sometimes the best way to teach your child about the Catholic faith is to show them by example, or to talk without using words. By simply spending time with you as you demonstrate love and other Christlike qualities, she can learn a great deal about who Jesus is and what it means to love and serve God. Make quality family time a regular practice and model Christian behavior and prayer. Over time, you will likely find your child coming to *you* to initiate conversations about God and your religious beliefs. As St. Francis said: "Preach the gospel daily. If necessary, use words."

TO SUPPORT YOU

SUGGESTED BIBLE READING
As the people of God, we are like stones in a holy structure, held together by Christ: Ephesians 2:19–22

WHAT THE CHURCH SAYS ABOUT THIS TOPIC
There is a long tradition in Christianity that calls the family "the **domestic church.**" This is where children first learn about God and Jesus, how to love and forgive, and how to live and work together.

One of the best and most practical ways to strengthen the family structure is through the family dinner. In our age of fast food and eating on the go, we often find ourselves eating a meal in isolation. In the Bible, meals are seen as much more than a means to satisfy a physical need. The Hebrew people viewed eating a meal together as a way of expressing and strengthening their relationships with one another under God's **covenant.** This is why the Pharisees found it so scandalous for Jesus to eat with tax collectors and sinners (see Luke 5:27–32). In eating with the outcasts, Jesus was forming a relationship with them and bringing them into the covenant.

It is no coincidence that meals are often the setting of Jesus' teachings and miracles in the Gospels, for example the feeding of the five thousand by multiplying five loaves and two fish (Mark 6: 34–44). Likewise, Jesus used the imagery of a banquet as a metaphor for the kingdom (Luke 14:15). The cup that Jesus shared with his disciples at the Last Supper was a pledge of the cup he will share with them at their next banquet in the **kingdom of God.** In our families, praying before and after we eat together is an opportunity to make our meals a time of renewing our relationships with God and with one another.

A Prayer Moment with Your Child

Now let's pray to Jesus, giving thanks for our family and the love that they give us:

*Jesus, thank you for letting me be part of a special community
of love and prayer with my family.
Thank you for putting others in my life
so that together we may grow closer to you.
Amen*

16

Responding to a child who was lost or left waiting

Faith Themes

The Holy Spirit guides our choices to help us live in peace.
Jesus teaches us to love, respect, and care for one another.

Natural Teachable Moments

- When you and your child are on the way to a large shopping center, amusement park, or other crowded area
- Before your child's first day at school or camp
- After your child or a sibling is lost and then found

THROUGH A MISCOMMUNICATION, A FIRST-GRADE BOY WAS LEFT ALONE after school on his first day. He did not know where to go or what to do. As his older sister was leaving school, she suddenly wondered whether her brother might be alone and confused. She went to his classroom, found him, and walked home with him. Her care and concern for her brother helped her to respond instinctively to his need for help. It is in moments such as this that we discover God alive in our family relationships. But those moments do not just happen. They are based on the daily practice of prayer, on centering our lives on Jesus, and following where the **Holy Spirit** leads us.

Starting the Conversation

Has anyone in you family been lost and then found? Has this happened to you, whether physically or spiritually? Share stories with your child and assure him of your constant protection and guidance. Affirm him in the knowledge that the Holy Spirit—who is everywhere and has guided your child since **baptism**—will always be with him, even when he feels lost.

To Help You Pray

Although you want to teach your child that he can pray anytime and anywhere, you may also want him to know prayer as something other than the hurried, task-oriented communication that makes up much of our busy days with others. For a rich and full prayer life, making a special place for you and your child to pray together will show him how much you value prayer time and your relationship with God. Allowing your child to participate in choosing a special time and location and in preparing the area shows him how much you respect his spirituality and see him as a full person of faith. When creating a prayer center in your home, you want to foster an awareness of this as sacred space. This can be done as simply as marking the area with a cloth in the color of the church's liturgical season, by placing a Bible there, or by choosing together a crucifix, statue, icon, or other religious symbol for the area. Another common practice is to place a special candle there that you and your child can light together when you pray.

TO SUPPORT YOU

SUGGESTED BIBLE READING

All are asked to bear one another's burdens: Galatians 6:2

WHAT THE CHURCH SAYS ABOUT THIS TOPIC

Our entire religious tradition is centered on the importance of healthy relationships. At the beginning of the Old Testament we hear the divine statement that it is not good for us to be alone. God creates man and woman as companions. And when God intervenes in human history, it is to form descendants of **Abraham** into one people. They are given the **Ten Commandments,** which are aimed at fostering healthy relationships with God and with other people.

Jesus came in fulfillment of the Scriptures not as an isolated individual but as a member of a family. He taught his followers to regard God as their loving Father, and in doing so, he made it clear to them that they were all brothers and sisters. Throughout his public life, Jesus tried to teach his disciples all the things they would need to form healthy relationships.

Jesus introduced us to the **Trinity** as well, the mystery of three persons in one God. Thus, the value we place on our relationships goes deeper than tradition or a desire for harmony and well-being: it is rooted in the very nature of God.

A Prayer Moment with Your Child

Now, with the Holy Spirit's help, let's thank Jesus for being our example of how to live as a loving person:

Jesus, thank you for showing me how good it is
to share your love with my family and with others.
Help me to always be aware of those who need me
so that I can serve others as you did.
Help me to follow what the Holy Spirit is telling me to do.
Amen

17

Sharing another person's company

Faith Themes

Jesus works through us to reach all people.
Jesus is with us through love and in a special way through the sacraments.

Natural Teachable Moments

- When going to visit grandparents or when a favorite relative is coming to stay
- When your child's new friend makes a big impression on her
- When you tell your child that she will be having a sitter or time with your spouse because you will be out with a friend

MANY OF US WONDER WHAT IT WOULD HAVE BEEN LIKE TO MEET JESUS in person. We would have liked to hear him speak and to experience his healing touch. The writers of the Gospels felt the same way. When the Gospels were written, two or three generations had passed since Jesus' life, death, and resurrection. People were feeling more removed from Jesus. The writer of the book of Luke dealt with the issue by telling the story of the Roman officer who had asked Jesus to heal his servant from a distance. He trusted that Jesus' healing power would overcome any limitations. In response, Jesus healed the servant and praised the officer for his faith. Luke's Gospel is telling us that Jesus is alive and still with us. Through his resurrection and ascension Jesus lives with his Father and shares his continuing presence with us—in a special way through the **sacraments,** and through the love we have for one another.

Starting the Conversation

It is easy to forget that we meet Jesus in one another. Ask your child what person she encountered today who made Jesus more present, perhaps through the joy the person brought into your child's life or the love that person shared or the patience he or she exhibited. Share your own experience as well.

To Help You Pray

As you mentor your child in prayer, guide her to know that she can strengthen her personal relationship with God by praying almost anywhere. Prayer does not have to occur in church, at the dining table, or with hands folded while kneeling at the bedside. Prayer can occur while riding the bus to school, walking the dog, taking a shower, or helping someone carry groceries. Prayer can happen when fear strikes or when we are looking into the face of a loved one. Your child can pray just about anywhere and at anytime. Let her know that prayer happens whenever she becomes aware of God's presence and shares her own presence with God. God is everywhere, so she can pray everywhere. Prayer can involve words, but it does not have to. Prayer can also be silent listening, meditative reflection that uses the imagination, or simply the feeling of being embraced by God's presence.

TO SUPPORT YOU

SUGGESTED BIBLE READING

Jesus tells the Pharisees that the **kingdom of God** is already here: Luke 17:21

WHAT THE CHURCH SAYS ABOUT THIS TOPIC

Jesus is present with us when we love others as God loves, and he is present when others love us. Jesus is also present with us, in a special way, in the Catholic Church's seven sacraments. In each of the sacraments, Jesus reaches out to touch our lives. For example, he touches us with new life in **baptism,** with forgiveness in **penance,** with love in **matrimony,** and with nourishment in the **Eucharist.**

The sacraments are outward signs of the grace we receive from God. In the sacraments we celebrate this grace. The actions and rituals of the sacraments do not earn us God's grace; they express that we acknowledge God's grace, celebrate it, and enjoy it.

The sacraments are not to be confused with **sacramentals.** Sacramentals are signs created by the church to help us in our devotional life. These include physical objects such as **holy water.** They also include gestures such as the **laying on of hands** and **blessings.** The word *sacramental* also encompasses objects such as statues, rosaries, scapulars, medals, and other objects, and actions that remind us of God's presence in our everyday lives. Sacramentals such as these have their origins in church tradition and prepare us to receive God's grace and the fruits of the sacrament, meaning the good things that the sacrament yields.

A Prayer Moment with Your Child

Let's pray now to Jesus, who is with us always:
Dear Jesus, thank you for giving me the sacraments
and the people in my life who love me.
Help me to be open to the grace of the Holy Spirit,
so I can show my love for God and others.
Amen

18

Showing concern for the poor and weak

Faith Themes

St. Katharine Drexel followed the Spirit.
When we work with God we receive the fruits of the Holy Spirit.

Natural Teachable Moments

- When your family makes plans to do service work together
- When your child watches a movie, TV show, or news program about a disturbing example of social injustice
- When you, your spouse, or another significant adult in your child's life changes jobs to do something that helps people or that is more in line with a calling to ministry

KATHARINE DREXEL (1858–1955) WAS BORN INTO A WEALTHY FAMILY in Pennsylvania. Her parents taught her that with great wealth came responsibility. After Katharine's parents died, she traveled around the country and saw the suffering of many people, especially Native Americans and African Americans. She decided to use her fortune to help them. On a visit to Rome, Katharine was granted a meeting with Pope Leo XIII. She asked the pope to send missionaries to help those who were poor. The pope replied, "Why don't *you* become a missionary?" Katharine realized she was being challenged to do more. Katharine responded to the challenge of the pope and the call of the Holy Spirit by dedicating her life to people in need.

When she returned to America, Katharine started an order called the Sisters of the Blessed Sacrament, and thereafter she committed her life to being "the mother and servant" of the Native and African American peoples. Spending millions of her own money, she began about sixty schools and social centers for Native American children in the West and for African American children in the rural and large urban areas of the southern United States. In 1915, Katharine and her fellow sisters founded Xavier University in New Orleans—the first U.S. Catholic institution of higher learning for African Americans. She also worked to feed and clothe poor people. Katharine Drexel died in 1955, and Pope John Paul II canonized her as a saint on October 1, 2000.

Starting the Conversation

Katharine Drexel learned about responsibility from her parents. Discuss with your child ways in which you and your family can responsibly assist less fortunate people in your community.

To Help You Connect

The story of Katharine Drexel can be unsettling to some parents who are unsure about encouraging their children to serve or work with the poor, sick, aged, or other people marginalized by society: "Katharine gave up her wealth—if my child does this, won't he be in need, uncomfortable, less secure?" The important part of the story to remember is that Katharine acted according to the movements of the **Holy Spirit**, and thus she became a coworker with God in what she was doing. Being with God in this manner releases one from fears, affords God's protection, and brings a sense of peace and fulfillment to the depths of a person's soul.

Also keep in mind that responsibly assisting others means that we help where and when we are needed, as directed by the Spirit. To do this we must listen carefully to the Spirit within us, for we are not called to every mission on this earth, just the one set out for us. Nor does service mean harming ourselves in order to help others—for we are called to love ourselves as well—but it means standing in solidarity and in spirit with the poor and the marginalized. With this understanding, you can confidently encourage your child to follow where the Holy Spirit leads him.

TO SUPPORT YOU

SUGGESTED BIBLE READING

The fruits of the Holy Spirit are listed: Galatians 5:22–23

WHAT THE CHURCH SAYS ABOUT THIS TOPIC

The biblical root of the word *Spirit* is *ruah,* which means "breath" or "wind." The Holy Spirit indicates God's activity in the world. God's activity is symbolized in the New Testament as a strong wind, tongues of fire, or a descending dove. The emphasis of these images is on their unpredictable, unrestricted movement, because the Spirit is the "animator" of God's will and of our acts when we follow the Spirit.

When Jesus sent the Holy Spirit to his disciples at Pentecost, the Spirit was symbolized as tongues of flames above each disciple's head. It signified the disciples' calling to go into the world and carry out Jesus' mission.

Jesus not only sent the Holy Spirit to the early followers of his church, but he also sends the Spirit to us today—to be with us and to guide us. The Holy Spirit works inside us, helping us grow stronger in our faith. When we listen to the Spirit and allow the Spirit to guide our actions, the **fruits of the Holy Spirit** result: love, patience, kindness, joy, peace, gentleness, generosity, faithfulness, and self-control. These fruits are seen in our actions, meaning that we find ourselves acting in these ways because we are cooperating with the Holy Spirit.

A Prayer Moment with Your Child

We know how important the Holy Spirit was in the growth of the early church and still is in our lives today. Let's thank Jesus for sending us the Holy Spirit:

Jesus, my helper, thank you for sending the Holy Spirit
to support me on my journey.
Help me to appreciate the presence of the Spirit in my life.
Amen

19

Dealing with doubt and distrust

Faith Themes

Adam and Eve's distrust of God had lasting effects on the human condition. God promised to send us a savior, Jesus Christ.

Natural Teachable Moments

- When your child struggles to believe in God
- When a tragedy occurs in your child's world, and she views God or the world with suspicion or fear
- When your child has done something wrong and doesn't seem to care

THE STORY OF ADAM AND EVE IS ONE WE ALL KNOW WELL. What we tend to forget amid the images of the garden, the forbidden fruit, and the serpent is that theirs is a story about a lack of trust in God and its effect on the human condition. This story illustrates that not trusting God and instead following our temptations always leads us to pain and suffering; we have less and are less than when we fully trusted in God. When we lose our trust in God, we also become less able to trust in one another.

The TV has made all of us witnesses to what happens in the world because of distrust. Our children will experience doubt, disappointment, and anxiety—in school and in their relationships with friends. As parents, we can feel quite helpless when confronting these issues. Yet in the midst of the disorder Adam and Eve created when they sinned, God promised a savior. This promise was fulfilled in Jesus Christ. Even in the disorder of our world and our individual lives, we can be examples to our children of what it means to live in the saving presence of Jesus.

Starting the Conversation

When events in the world dominate the conversation, listen attentively to the concerns of your child, and answer her questions honestly. Is she feeling fear or mistrust? Anxiety or sadness? Perhaps indifference or coldness of heart? Resist any urge to judge your child, but instead suggest a time to pray together for the needs of the world and about anything that frightens or worries her.

To Help You Pray

Talk with your child about the importance of praying often, even when it seems that God is not listening or when we doubt God. Let your child know she can say *anything* to God, ask for anything, pray about anything or for anyone—all she has to do is express what is in her heart. God already sees what is in our hearts, so there is nothing to hide, and because God loves us unconditionally, there is nothing to fear. Invite your child to pray with you, and ask what she would like to pray for today.

TO SUPPORT YOU

SUGGESTED BIBLE READING

Adam and Eve sin, and humanity falls from grace: Genesis 3:1–24

WHAT THE CHURCH SAYS ABOUT THIS TOPIC

Chapter 3 of Genesis tells us how man and woman's intimate relationship with God and each other was disrupted. In the beginning in the garden, everything and everyone was in harmony. Then the serpent misled Adam and Eve by telling them that God had forbidden them to eat from a certain tree because it would give them God's knowledge of good and evil. Adam and Eve listened to the serpent and not to God; thus, their fundamental sin was a lack of trust in God.

The consequence of their disobedience was immediate. The innocence of Adam and Eve was shattered, and they became aware of their nakedness. Their intimate relationship with God was broken, and they hid in fear when God came to walk with them in the garden. Their sin also caused suffering. They had to leave the garden and enter a world of hard work and sorrow. Life without suffering, symbolized by the garden of intimacy and peace, was over.

Anyone who thinks that humans can create such a perfect place as the **Garden of Eden** without respect for God's moral order learns the same painful lesson that Adam and Eve learned. The story of Adam and Eve teaches us that we must trust in God and do God's will.

However, the story does not end there. God did not abandon Adam and Eve after their sin. God promised that salvation and forgiveness of sins would come through a savior. This promise was fulfilled in his son, Jesus Christ.

A Prayer Moment with Your Child

When we turn away from God, we hurt ourselves and others. Let's thank God for sending us a savior to help mend all our relationships:

Thank you, God, for sending us a savior
to mend our relationship with you.
Please help me mend my relationships with other people, too.
Amen

20

Communicating "You're okay!"

Faith Themes

The Holy Spirit helps us feel loved.
The Holy Spirit is God's active presence among us.

Natural Teachable Moments:

- When your child brings home a report card
- When your child has been teased by neighbors, friends, or family
- When you are teaching your child a new skill or activity

EVERYONE NEEDS APPROVAL. Feeling appreciated and liked is especially important in the life of a child. As parents, our words are extremely powerful because they help form our children's identities. When we think about this issue, it is helpful to remember and reflect on the people in *our* lives who helped us realize how important we are. Our hearts can skip a beat just thinking of their words of approval. This sense of well-being is one of the ways we recognize the depth of God's love for us. As our children come before us in fragility and hope, we must recognize the opportunity presented to us: discovering the individuals who the **Holy Spirit** is calling our children to be. What could be more valuable?

Starting the Conversation

Share with your child something you recall about a person who was important to you. What did this person say or do that made such an impression on you? Talk together about people who are important in your child's life. Are there similarities between your child's influences and your own?

To Help You Ask Questions

When asking your child to share, remember to speak from your heart. Your child can sense whether you *really* want to hear his answer or whether you are just going through the motions. Try not to speak too rapidly, and pause after asking a question. Your silence will let your child know that you really are ready to listen and are waiting for his response. If he puts you off or simply answers, "I don't know," ask the question again, in an encouraging tone, and then pause again, until he responds more meaningfully.

TO SUPPORT YOU

SUGGESTED BIBLE READING
Jesus empowers the disciples with the Holy Spirit to continue his mission: John 20:19–22

WHAT THE CHURCH SAYS ABOUT THIS TOPIC
In the Gospel of John we are told how Jesus came to his disciples after his resurrection and gave them the gift of the Holy Spirit. In the Bible, *spirit* does not mean something unearthly, but rather God active and living in the world. The word for *spirit* in the Old Testament means "wind." The Holy Spirit is God active in the world and in our lives.

The Holy Spirit is the gift of God's peace from the Father and the Son. The Holy Spirit helps us know we are loved and helps us share this love with others. When we find ourselves treating others with compassion as Jesus did, we can recognize that we are moving in the Holy Spirit. When we recognize that we are personally loved, when we help others without being asked, and when we forgive those who hurt us, we are experiencing God's Holy Spirit. When we affirm our children and the individuals they are being called to become, we are acting in the Holy Spirit.

A Prayer Moment with Your Child

Let's take a moment to thank God for important people in our lives and for how they give us a sense of well-being and help us know we are loved:

God, thank you for the people in my life
who love me and support me.
Thank you for your gift of the Holy Spirit,
who helps me feel this love and brings me peace.
Amen

21

Coping with sibling rivalry

Faith Themes

Every child is special.
A Christian family's solidarity mirrors the solidarity of Christ's church.

Natural Teachable Moments:

- When your child is becoming overly competitive
- When your child feels that you or another family member favors a sibling over her, or when you find yourself making comparisons between your children
- When your child has trouble with a "teacher's pet" at school or a coach's favorite on a sports team

SIBLING RIVALRY IS COMMON IN ALL FAMILIES. For example, in one of the Bible's Old Testament stories, parents **Isaac and Rebecca** experienced this problem with their twin sons, **Jacob and Esau.** These two boys competed with each other from the day they were born. In fact, Esau was born first, and Jacob was born holding on to Esau's foot! They were completely different in looks and personality, and unfortunately their parents each favored a different son.

This probably made the brothers' competition worse. The two boys competed for their parents' affection and for the right to receive their father's blessing, a special right in Jewish custom reserved for the firstborn. Through trickery and with the help of their mother, Rebecca, Jacob gained his father Isaac's blessing but lost his family. He had to flee for his life when Esau sought revenge.

It is easy for parents to make comparisons between their children. The subtle hints convey that one child's behavior and gifts meet with approval while those of others somehow fall short. When you make any comparison among children in a way that sets them against one another, family solidarity is damaged. Each child is unique and blessed by God. Celebrate that uniqueness in noncompetitive ways.

Starting the Conversation

Mention to your child one gift that she brings to the family. Tell her that you and your family recognize how special she is to the family. Acknowledge that she is unique and irreplaceable.

To Help You Connect

When you mention gifts your child brings to the family, try to include a recent specific example. You may have a ready example of a gift, virtue, or talent. Or you may need to consider this for a few moments as you reflect on the past week. Even if what you come up with seems mundane or very obvious to you, it may not be mundane or obvious to your child. Yes, she may hear about her unique gifts and specialness from friends, at school, or in her religious education sessions at your parish, but she still needs to hear these things from *you*—the primary teacher in her life at this age.

TO SUPPORT YOU

SUGGESTED BIBLE READING
Jacob deceives his brother: Genesis 25:19–34 and 27:1–45

WHAT THE CHURCH SAYS ABOUT THIS TOPIC
When hearing the Bible story of Jacob manipulating Esau out of his birth-right and blessing, we may wonder why Isaac did not simply veto the twin's exchange and take back his special blessing from Jacob and give it Esau. To the ancient Jews, a birthright gave special power and entitlements and was so important that biblical law guaranteed it. When Esau gave his birthright away, he was not entitled to have it back. The **blessing** that Isaac gave Jacob was also permanent. A blessing was actually a request to God to confer blessings, and only God could give blessings. Isaac could bless—or, rather, ask God to bless—because he had a close relationship with God. Once Isaac asked for the blessing, he was unable to ask God to take away Jacob's blessing.

The story doesn't end there, however. The Bible goes on to tell how Jacob, having fled his family home and Esau's anger, got tricked himself. He had to work for a man for seven years longer than he had agreed to, in order to marry the man's daughter. Jacob sinned and experienced suffering, yet God did not abandon him. The story ends with God guiding Jacob to find his destiny: taking the new name Israel and being able to face the brother he had tricked years ago. Esau forgave Jacob, and their competition finally ended.

A Prayer Moment with Your Child
Let's thank God now for guiding us as he guided Jacob:
Loving God, thank you for being faithful to me
even when I sin.
Help me to trust in you
through everything that happens to me.
Amen

22

Recognizing the sacred in everyday life

Faith Themes

God is present in everyday life and invites us to be in his presence.
Jesus is the model of love and goodness for our lives.

Natural Teachable Moments

- When you and your child find some mundane thing suddenly amusing or entertaining
- During Ordinary Time in the church liturgical year
- When you and your child walk the dog, water flowers, visit a neighbor, cook, or perform another ordinary task

WE DON'T KNOW VERY MUCH ABOUT JESUS' LIFE ON EARTH. We know about his birth, a little about his infancy, and of one event when he was about twelve years old. Then we learn more about Jesus when he was about thirty. Details of Jesus' daily life are quite scarce. Like any Jewish boy of his time, Jesus learned the traditions of his people. He learned a trade. He obeyed his mother and father. Most of his days, like most of ours, were probably filled with the ordinary things that people do. The simplicity of his life shows us that ordinary days are grace-filled days. In the midst of his life, Jesus prepared for his mission.

God is also present in our everyday lives. In the loving families that we help God to nurture, in the relationships with our spouse and our children that we help God to fill with love, ordinary life becomes sacred. In this way, we become "coworkers" with God, imbuing daily life with sanctity and grace.

Starting the Conversation

Discuss a good deed that someone in your family observed today. Did someone help without being asked? Did someone share a snack or money without expectation of return? Did someone offer his or her presence to another in need of a listening ear or a shoulder to cry on? Did someone yield to another even though they had the right-of-way? What feeling or action did this deed inspire in you, your child, or other family member who witnessed it?

To Help You Connect

Make eye contact with your child when you talk with him. Studies have shown that making eye contact actually increases brain activity! Ample eye contact can assist you in conveying your message and your sincerity to your child. It will also help you better hold his attention and perceive nonverbal cues from him—such as whether or not he understands the conversation, whether he has a question to ask, or if he is engaged by, or withdrawing from, your talk. Be aware of signs of encouragement to continue, such as a smile or slight nod of the head, or signs of waning attention, such as wandering eyes.

TO SUPPORT YOU

SUGGESTED BIBLE READING

Jesus tells us he will be with us always: Matthew 28:20

WHAT THE CHURCH SAYS ABOUT THIS TOPIC

Jesus said to those who followed his teachings: "And Behold, I am with you always, until the end of the age." God is always with us and is constantly inviting us into a deeper and more freeing relationship with him. God uses every means possible—all of life—to accomplish this. Through the **Holy Spirit,** we can recognize and experience God's presence in our lives and choose how to respond to God's invitation. Christ's example of loving goodness here on earth is the model for our response.

Jesus, a compassionate man, teaches us to be concerned for the suffering of others and to do what we can to alleviate suffering. Jesus, the man of solidarity, teaches us to identify with people in need. The champion of the marginalized, Jesus wants us to stand with those who are forced to the fringes of society and to promote their causes. Jesus, the healer, teaches us to be reconcilers in society and in our families, and to promote physical, mental, and spiritual health. Jesus, the servant, shows us how to look out for the interests of others. The rescuer of the lost, Jesus teaches us to rescue people rather than judge them.

A Prayer Moment with Your Child

Let's thank Jesus for being our example of how to love God and others, and for being with us in the ordinary moments of our lives:

Thank you, Jesus, for showing me your loving ways,
so that I can share your love with others.
Help me recognize God's invitation to me in daily life
and to respond to it with openness and love.
Amen

23

Seeking forgiveness and healing

Faith Themes

God forgives us and heals our bodies and our souls.
The two sacraments of healing are penance and anointing of the sick.

Natural Teachable Moments

- After your child has a fight with a sibling or other child
- When your child witnesses you and your spouse or other family members quarreling
- When someone your child knows is gravely ill and is visited by a priest to be given last rites

On May 13, 1981, an attempt was made to assassinate the man who was then our pope, **John Paul II.** The injured pope was rushed to the hospital and underwent surgery for six hours. In his first public statement following the incident, he asked all to "pray for the brother who shot me, whom I have sincerely forgiven." Then he visited the prison cell of the person who shot him, and the pope repeated his words of forgiveness. Through his words and actions, the pope was an example of the healing grace of forgiveness.

Catholics receive this grace when we celebrate the **sacrament of penance,** one of the two **sacraments of healing.** Healing is not only about the physical body; a soul can be healed, too, through forgiveness. Have we done things we've regretted? Do we need forgiveness? Recognizing that God forgives us opens us to the grace with which we forgive others.

Starting the Conversation

Describe to your child a time when you forgave someone who had hurt you. Describe how it felt to forgive that person, and describe some of the results of that forgiveness. Ask your child how your family could become more forgiving in general.

To Help You Connect

When discussing forgiveness with your child, you may want to acknowledge that forgiving someone who has harmed you can be very difficult. Sometimes we view what the other person or persons did to us as really, really bad—and we don't *want* to forgive them. We may think they do not deserve forgiveness, and we may find ourselves holding on to our hurts and resentments. In the end, though, withholding forgiveness only harms us more. It perpetuates the injury and delays our own healing. It can be difficult to forgive another, but through God we have the strength to do so. We are able to forgive others, through God's grace, when we remember that we, too, are sinners who need God's forgiveness again and again.

TO SUPPORT YOU

SUGGESTED BIBLE READING

Jesus sends forth his disciples to heal: Luke 9:1–6

WHAT THE CHURCH SAYS ABOUT THIS TOPIC

In the book of Luke, we read about how Jesus summoned the twelve apostles and gave them the mission to spread the good news of God's saving love. He also granted them the authority to heal the sick—physically and spiritually—as he had done. What Jesus gave to his disciples, he also gives to people today through the church. That includes healing gifts.

We can be sick in a number of ways, and the Catholic Church provides us with healing aids for all of our sicknesses. There are two sacraments of healing: **penance** and the **anointing of the sick.** When we are physically sick from injury or disease, the sacrament of anointing of the sick heals our psychological and spiritual suffering and, if it is God's will, can provide physical healing. When we are morally or spiritually ill, the sacrament of penance heals by providing forgiveness from God and from the community. When we are not psychologically healthy, because of such things as depression or addiction, the sacraments of healing provide us with the strength of God's grace so that we can experience psychological healing.

A Prayer Moment with Your Child

Let's take a moment to thank Jesus for always wanting to help us:
Jesus, thank you for healing me in every way.
Help me to turn to you when I need my body or my spirit to be healed.
Amen

24

Beginning the week with "family Sunday"

Faith Themes

Going to Mass and honoring the Sabbath help unite families.
The celebration of the Eucharist is the center of parish life.

Natural Teachable Moments

- On the way home from Sunday Mass
- During a family dinner
- When your child expresses enjoyment of a family activity or some past family event

CELEBRATING MASS IS CENTRAL TO OUR LIVES AS CATHOLICS. It is the celebration of our union with Jesus Christ and with one another. We celebrate that union best as a family when we create time for one another. On Sunday morning, try to eliminate the ordinary distractions. Keep the TV set, video games, and headphones off. Do some things differently, such as walking to church instead of driving. Arrange to have a special meal. Set aside some time for rest time, in which you have no plans and specific work to do except to just "be" and to see what happens. Building family unity at home strengthens your union with Jesus.

Starting the Conversation

As a family, plan what you can do together to make Sunday different from any other day of the week. Tell your child of your desire to start the week off in some special way together. Ask him what he suggests that everyone could do to honor the day as a family.

To Help You Listen

Listen closely to your child's ideas of what your family can do on Sundays and, if possible, commit to him that you will discuss his idea with others in the family. Let him know that you will get back to him about his suggestion by the following Saturday or another specific day. One of the more unconstructive things a parent can do is ask for a child's suggestions about family activities and then never respond one way or another to his ideas. If your child's idea is unrealistic, try to come up with a similar yet practical alternative that is still in the same sphere as your child's suggestion. And if he offers an idea that is inappropriate for a Sunday activity, gently explain that things that would honor family Sundays are those that reflect God's love for us all. And then be sure to invite him to try again.

TO SUPPORT YOU

SUGGESTED BIBLE READING

An account of Jesus and the disciples celebrating the **Last Supper:** 1 Corinthians 11:23–26

WHAT THE CHURCH SAYS ABOUT THIS TOPIC

The celebration of the **Eucharist** is not a private devotion but rather a communal gathering, much like a family meal. We come together at the same time and in the same place so that we can take part in a common action. We open with a ceremony of pardoning, a way to unburden ourselves of past offenses so that we can rejoice in one another's company. Later we share a **sign of peace** and reconciliation. We don't sit and read the Bible quietly to ourselves but rather listen to it proclaimed to us as a community. We follow this with a public proclamation of our faith.

Then we gather around the table of the Lord for our family meal. As we prepare to eat our meal, we pray the **Lord's Prayer,** the prayer that has identified and united Christians for centuries. The actual partaking of the food is referred to as "communion," a joining together of the members of the community, not only with their God but also with one another. Jesus is with us in the Eucharist, which is the **real presence** of Jesus Christ in the appearance of bread and wine. This presence is real, not merely figurative or symbolic. Our celebration closes with a charge to go forth as a community and bring God's love to the world.

A Prayer Moment with Your Child

Let's take a few moments to pray together to Jesus:

Thank you, Jesus, for making Sundays a special day
to be with you in the Mass.
Thank you for my family
and for making me one with God's family
when I go to celebrate Mass.
Amen

25

Learning or choosing names

Faith Themes

A person's name has spiritual importance.
Jesus renamed Peter and gave us leaders in the church.

Natural Teachable Moments

- When your family is choosing the name for a new pet
- When your child makes a friend with an uncommon name
- When your child asks what your or another family member's middle name is or why

CHOOSING A NAME FOR A CHILD TAKES THOUGHT. On the day of the September 11, 2001, tragedy, one couple named their newborn son Lucas. They did so because the name means "bringer of light." His name was a prayer for him and for the world, too. Jesus also knew the importance of names. He saw in Simon the person of strength he needed to lead his disciples. So Jesus renamed Simon, calling him **Peter,** which means "rock," the rock on which Jesus could build the church. Peter, a man who loved greatly and sometimes failed miserably, was also capable of change and growth. He was the kind of man Jesus needed.

Starting the Conversation

Jesus saw Peter as a "rock." Ask your child what image Jesus would use to describe individual members of your family in regard to their mission in God's kingdom. The heart? The doorway? The mountain? The rainbow? The lighthouse? Why?

To Help You Ask Questions

Before asking your child what Jesus might name the members of your family in relation to their role for God, you may want to share how and why you chose *her* first or middle name. If she was named after a family member, share what that person meant to you and why. If they are Christian names, you may tell your child who that biblical person or saint was and read together about her life (resources and websites for this are listed in the back of this book). You may start by saying, "Honey, did I ever tell you why we chose to name you . . . ?" Or you may explain the reasons for your own name or the names of others in the family. Then ask what gifts and strengths Jesus might see in people of your family today, and how he would name them in regard to those gifts and strengths.

TO SUPPORT YOU

Suggested Bible Reading

Jesus renames Peter and gives him authority to head the church:
Matthew 16:18–19

What the Church Says about This Topic

Many of the names in the Bible have special meaning, because the **Holy Spirit** guided the giving of the names. For example, the name *Peter* means "rock."

Jesus renamed Simon this because he knew Peter would be a strong leader of the church. The name *Jesus* means "God saves." An angel told **Joseph** in a dream to name **Mary's** baby this because the child would save his people from their sins. *Christ* is a title that means "anointed with oil." It is from a Greek word that means the same thing as the Hebrew word *Messiah,* or "anointed." It is the name given to Jesus after the Resurrection when he completed his mission as priest, prophet, and king. The word *Christian* means "follower of Christ." In the Acts of the Apostles, we learn that Christ's followers were first called Christians in the town of Antioch, after the church had been established there (Acts 11:26).

This tradition was continued in the early church. For example, St. Benedict's name means "blessed." A benediction is a **blessing.** The church's current pope, Benedict XVI, chose this as his new name when he became pope, following a tradition of renaming. Each pope chooses a new name that represents the new person he is becoming as head of the church. Letting the Holy Spirit guide the choosing of a name is a tradition that continues today in many places in the world.

A Prayer Moment with Your Child

Let's take some time to thank Jesus for our birth, our name, and the unique role each of us is asked to play in the life of the church:

Jesus, thank you for calling me to your church.
Support me as I follow your teachings
and let the Holy Spirit guide me
to become the person God the Father created me to be.
Amen

26

Praying for someone's needs

Faith Themes

It is our privilege and responsibility to pray for our children.
St. Monica gave us an example of faithfulness in prayer.

Natural Teachable Moments

- When someone your child knows is sick, has just received bad news about his or her health, or is experiencing misfortune
- When someone your child knows is making bad decisions and courting trouble
- When your child observes or reflects on poor, vulnerable, and unjustly treated people in this world

MONICA (332–387) WAS A CHRISTIAN BORN IN TAGASTE, a city in what is now Algeria. She married an official who was not Christian, Patricius, and they had three children. Monica lived as an exemplary Christian and encouraged her family to do the same so that they could experience the peace of Jesus' love. Her husband and two of her children, Perpetua and Navigius, were baptized and became Christians. However, her third child, **Augustine,** proved more difficult to guide in a Christian life. Augustine made bad decisions and pursued a worldly lifestyle. During that time, Monica loved and prayed for her son. Before she died, she finally witnessed his conversion and saw him baptized at the age of thirty-three. Augustine went on to become a bishop, a great Christian writer, and a saint himself.

Monica, the patron saint of married women and a model for Christian mothers, is a great example of persistence and faithfulness in prayer. As parents we recognize in St. Monica a kindred spirit who prays with us that our children may make good choices and turn toward Jesus.

Starting the Conversation

Share with your child that one of the best ways we can help those in need is to pray. Explain that in our prayers we don't just pray *for* those in need, we pray *about* them. When praying for people, it's possible to form an aloof separateness between those persons and yourself, but in order to pray about people, you must acknowledge your inherent connection with them and their meaning to you personally. We remember that, like us, those in need are children of God and deserve dignity, love, and respect.

To Help You Pray

Sharing prayer time with your child in reverence and sincerity is the best way to model that each of us is called to develop our own personal relationship with God. Before you pray together, talk with your child about the place of prayer in your life. Begin prayer by inviting him to still his heart and mind so as to focus quietly on God's presence with him right now. If you are praying a traditional or written prayer, speak slowly, with reverence, and contemplate each word's meaning. If you are leading your child in a reflective prayer in your own words, speak slowly, with feeling, and pause often so that he can reflect on what you're saying. And at the end of your prayer time, be sure to give your child a few moments to pray silently in his heart.

TO SUPPORT YOU

SUGGESTED BIBLE READING

Paul writes a letter of joy and prays unceasingly for the early Christian community: Philippians 1:1–11

WHAT THE CHURCH SAYS ABOUT THIS TOPIC

Even when her son Augustine was far away and rejecting her efforts to guide him, St. Monica never stopped praying for him. She had hope for her son and trust in God, and she believed that Augustine would one day choose to follow Jesus. She was steadfast in her prayer and in modeling Christian behavior, and her son eventually was moved to accept Christ.

Likewise, when St. Paul was far from the members of his Christian family, he, too, trusted in God to keep them safe and to keep their faith strong. He wrote letters to the early Christian communities, thanking God for them, expressing his joy in them, and urging them to pray for one another. When writing a letter to the Christians in Philippi, St. Paul was in jail—put there by officials who did not want him spreading Jesus' message—but he was praying unceasingly for *them*. Because Paul, in the letter that became the biblical book Philippians, rejoices in the faith of the Christian community in Philippi, this letter is sometimes known as "the letter of joy."

A Prayer Moment with Your Child

Let's pray to God now, sharing with him our thanks, needs, and hopes, and then listening quietly to the Holy Spirit in our hearts:
God, thank you for always listening to me
and speaking to me in my prayers.
Help me make prayer a priority in my life every day.
Amen

27

Embracing the goodness of the world

Faith Themes

God says that the world is good.

God created everything out of love for us; all of creation is good.

Natural Teachable Moments

- When your child asks "Why is . . . ?" or "Why does . . . ?" about the world
- When your child fears that the world may really be just a bad or ugly place
- After you and your child have heard or watched some particularly bad news in the media

CHILDREN LOVE SURPRISES. They soak up new experiences every day and ask many *why* questions about the way things work. But practical, scientific explanations for things aren't always enough. Sometimes children need to hear the spiritual meanings behind what they see. For example, when asked, "Why does a rainbow come out after the rain?" sometimes it's appropriate to tell the story of the rainbow (Genesis 9:13–17) and that it's a reminder of how God loves us and will never leave us.

In the Bible, the first chapter of Genesis is filled with this kind of wonder. God is the great craftsperson who created the sun, moon, and stars and said that they were very good. Perhaps even more amazingly, God keeps everything going day after day, and we awake each morning to see that God is doing it again. Children are God's happy surprises, too, and they remind us not to take anything for granted.

Starting the Conversation

Share memories of a time when your family discovered something wonderful or beautiful about the world. Share with your child how this discovery made you feel or how it changed you. Ask your child about a discovery of her own.

To Help You Connect

You can share a discovery that you made together as a family, such as a different custom or tradition you were introduced to during a family vacation. Or consider sharing a story from your own childhood—perhaps about a discovery you made when you were about the same age your child is now. A simple way to start is, "Did I ever tell you about the time when . . . ?"

TO SUPPORT YOU

SUGGESTED BIBLE READING

God creates **heaven** and earth and people: Genesis 1:1–31

WHAT THE CHURCH SAYS ABOUT THIS TOPIC

God created the universe and everything in it for us. Genesis 1:31 says that God proclaimed everything he made "very good." In the book of Genesis, the goodness of things is described concretely, in terms of ripe fields of grain ready for harvest. The world is for people to enjoy and use, but it is not to be exploited.

We are made in God's image and likeness, as living representatives of God on earth. As God's representatives, the human family has been given dominion over the earth. Human dominion is to be modeled on God's dominion. God's dominion respects life. We can begin to appreciate the goodness and beauty of God by appreciating the goodness and beauty of the created world.

The church teaches that God—the Father, the Son, and the **Holy Spirit**—creates, sustains, and loves all of creation. The created world is the result of God's decision to share his life and love with us. Should God forget the universe and everyone in it for an instant, it would lapse into nothingness.

A Prayer Moment with Your Child

Just as God's cares for us, we should care for God's creation. Let's thank God for the beautiful world he made and ask for his help to respect all its wonders:

Thank you, God, for all you have made.
Help me to love more by taking care of your creation.
Amen

28

Working with the concept of unconditional love

Faith Themes

God loves each person infinitely, eternally, and without condition.
We reflect God's love in our relationships with one another when we love unconditionally and forgive one another.

Natural Teachable Moments:

- After your child fails a test or gets into trouble at school
- When you and your child witness road rage
- When your child sees others make fun of children or adults who look "different" or when he makes fun of someone different

A SHEPHERD'S LIFE DURING JESUS' TIME WAS LONELY AND DIFFICULT. The wealth of the family was tied up in a flock that could easily be lost to a drought, a storm, a freezing night, or an attack from a predatory animal. With so much at stake, the idea of a shepherd's leaving the flock unprotected to look for one lost sheep seemed ridiculous. Yet that is the image Jesus uses in the Scriptures for the Father's love for us. Jesus wanted to emphasize the complete commitment that God makes to each one of us. God's love is a total, will-go-to-the-ends-of-the-universe-for-us kind of love. When we make wrong choices, God calls us back. God welcomes us with open arms, as the loving father does in the **parable of the prodigal son and the forgiving father.** Jesus especially waits for us to celebrate God's forgiveness in the **sacrament of penance** and reconciliation.

Starting the Conversation

Ask your child about a time when he felt surrounded by total love. Explain that God's love for him is like that—and more.

To Help You Connect

When talking to your child about God's infinite, unconditional love for him, you may need to better explain the word *unconditional.* This term is used so often in our society in partially appropriate ways that some of the power to convey its true meaning has been lost. Unconditional love is a love your child does not earn—and doesn't have to. It's a gift, freely given by God. Your child can't deserve it or not deserve it. There is nothing he can do to lose it. He can only respond to it. How your child chooses to respond is up to him. By returning the love? Ignoring God's love? Rejecting God? Running away? While sharing these ideas, you also may want to explain that God's love is infinite, meaning that it will never run out. As much as God gives us, there is always much more.

TO SUPPORT YOU

SUGGESTED BIBLE READING

Jesus tells the parable of the prodigal son and the forgiving father: Luke 15:11–24

WHAT THE CHURCH SAYS ABOUT THIS TOPIC

Understanding the context of Jesus' parable of the prodigal son and the forgiving father in the book of Luke makes its meaning richer for us. In the culture of Jesus' time, the father's behavior of welcoming his son back was very unusual. The father had been treated badly by his younger son, who asked for his share of the family estate while his father was still alive—tantamount to acting as if his father was already dead. Then the son squandered his father's gifts and provisions. By welcoming the son back with open arms, the father risked looking foolish in the eyes of his family, his workers, and his contemporaries.

Also, the father was filled with joy at his son's return and ran to embrace him, something a dignified man of the time would seldom do. This is precisely the point of the parable: God's joy in us is so great that God is willing to look "foolish" in welcoming back a sinner into a relationship with him.

A Prayer Moment with Your Child

Though we try not to, we sometimes sin; so let's thank God for his great love and the forgiveness he gives us:

God, thank you for your great and infinite love.
You never forget me,
and you call me back to you when I sin.
Help me repent and change
so that I may enjoy and return your love.
Amen

29

Healing injured relationships

Faith Themes

Jesus forgave Zacchaeus and dined with him.
By celebrating the sacrament of penance, we are reconciled with God and others.

Natural Teachable Moments

- After you and your spouse decide to reinitiate or repair a broken relationship with a relative or neighbor
- When your child has teased, injured, fought with, or stolen from a person in the community
- When your child becomes selfish or unwilling to share with others

When our children hurt one another, we can feel discouraged. We know that even though apologies are given and accepted, resentment can remain. In the Bible, Luke presents an account of reconciliation in the story of **Zacchaeus,** a tax collector who had taken advantage of, and stolen from, the Jewish people, and whom the people hated. Jesus did not scold Zacchaeus when they met, but rather asked Zacchaeus to invite him to dinner. In the Jewish tradition, sharing a meal with someone means you are reconciled and at peace with that person. Jesus' eating with Zacchaeus meant that Jesus forgave him and accepted him. Zacchaeus responded to Jesus' loving forgiveness by vowing to pay back everyone he had cheated. Jesus teaches us that we can help our children be reconciled with God and with one another. For example, the family dinner gives us a great opportunity to share conversation and build better relationships.

Starting the Conversation

Arrange a time to invite to dinner someone with whom your family or your child needs to rebuild a relationship. Discuss with your child beforehand why you are inviting this person (or persons) to dinner and what you hope to achieve by this. Ask your child to help you think of ways to make this experience more personal, comfortable, and enjoyable for your guest. Perhaps by cooking his or her favorite food? By inviting along the person's parents, spouse, or another significant individual?

To Help You Listen

For this discussion, and for all your conversations with your child, explain that you are always ready to listen to her, no matter what she would like to tell you, good or bad. Tell her that her honesty is more important to you than any mistake she might have made or wrong she might have done. Be sure not to criticize her when she is honest. Instead, thank her for telling the truth, and discuss what she should do now to make amends if needed or to do in the future to act according to Jesus' teaching.

TO SUPPORT YOU

Suggested Bible Reading

Jesus associates with and forgives a public sinner: Luke 19:2–9

What the Church Says about This Topic

When talking to your child about repentance, forgiveness, and reconciliation, spiritual concepts such as **heaven, hell,** and **purgatory** often come up. Avoid presenting heaven, hell, and purgatory as places; the Catholic faith teaches that they are three states of being. Heaven is the state of eternal happiness in union with God. Hell is the state of complete separation from God for all eternity; it is experienced by those who decide to reject God. Purgatory is the state of final preparation for those who are saved but not yet ready to be with God. In this temporary state, those damaged by sin are surrounded by divine love so that they can return to God in the original, perfect condition in which he created them.

Performing acts of **penance** and making **restitution** to those who we have wronged help us remove the effects of sin while we are on this earth. The church teaches that there are also ways to remove some of the damage of sin while people are in purgatory. **Indulgences** received while we are alive can help remove some of the effects of sin in purgatory. An indulgence is a prayer or practice approved by the church to reduce the effects of sin on a soul. Indulgences can be received by those who wish to pray for themselves. Indulgences may also be performed for the benefit of souls in purgatory so that they may more quickly enter into heaven.

A Prayer Moment with Your Child

Remember, God wants us to be at peace with him and with others. He gives us the wonderful gift of forgiveness and reconciliation. Let's thank Jesus for forgiving us and ask him to help us forgive others in the future:

Dear Jesus, thank you for helping me forgive others,
as you have forgiven me.
Help me become friends again with people who have hurt me
or whom I have hurt, so we can all experience greater peace.
Amen

30

Keeping promises and commitments

Faith Themes

God is committed to us and wants our commitment.
Using the Ten Commandments to guide our actions, we make good moral decisions and stay faithful to God.

Natural Teachable Moments

- When making your New Year's resolutions or explaining to your child what these are
- When your child attends a wedding or a renewal-of-vows ceremony
- When your child is preparing to receive a sacrament

THE DRAMATIC STORY OF THE ISRAELITES' ESCAPE FROM SLAVERY IN EGYPT and their receiving of the **Ten Commandments** is a biblical favorite of many children. What we should not overlook, however, amid the images of the Red Sea parting and the people wandering in a desert for forty years, is the great gift God gave to the Jewish people in the Ten Commandments. The Ten Commandments are a **covenant** God made with his people—the Jewish people then and God's church today. The commandments show us how to live in relationship with God and with one another. They are the foundation of the biblical teachings on justice and peace.

God made a commitment and will keep it. When we make commitments to our children, we can remember to model our promises on God's commitment to us. We recognize that we are called to keep faith with our children, as God keeps faith with us.

Starting the Conversation

What commitment to God would you and your child like to make? Will you promise to provide time for daily family prayer, to attend **Mass** together every Sunday, to help out at a local nursing home, or to read a children's Bible or other spiritual book at bedtime? Ask your child what promise he would like to make that will help him grow closer to God.

To Help You Listen

It's important to remember that when you ask your child a question, you owe him the respect of listening to his answer. If you have already decided what commitment to God you and your child can handle right now, then it is best not to ask for suggestions but to say what's already on your mind. In this case, gauge your child's enthusiasm and be prepared if he is not fully on board with what you're proposing. Always try to bear in mind that what you really want in these interactions is *two-way* conversation about things that matter—not just checking off of an item on a mental to-do list. Given the chance, our children's faith and creativity will often surprise us.

TO SUPPORT YOU

SUGGESTED BIBLE READING
God delivers the Ten Commandments through Moses: Exodus 20:1–17

WHAT THE CHURCH SAYS ABOUT THIS TOPIC

The Ten Commandments are part of God's revelation to us. We believe that God presented them to Moses atop Mount Sinai as essential rules to be followed. Many other cultures have lists of rules similar to the Ten Commandments. This is not surprising, as the essential teaching of the commandments is grounded in human nature and the **natural law.** Natural law is the innate moral sense given to us by God that enables us to discern between good and evil, what truth is and what a lie is.

Nevertheless, there is uniqueness to the Ten Commandments as revealed by God. Only in the Ten Commandments do we find a strict adherence to faith in one God and to the importance of God above all human actions and concerns. The Ten Commandments are also unparalleled because they are the foundation for the building of a covenant relationship between God and his people. A covenant is a solemn agreement between God and humanity, one that God will never break. People are called to obey the commandments as the way to be faithful in return to a loving God.

A Prayer Moment with Your Child

Let's pray together, thanking God for the rules of life he gave us—and the promise that following these rules will bring us eternal peace with God:

God, thank you for giving us your commandments
and for always keeping your promises.
With the help of the Holy Spirit, I want to follow your rules
because they lead to freedom and give me life.
Amen

31

Feeling left out
or just "not in"

Faith Themes

God is with his people, even in exile.
God gives comfort and hope to those who are outcast and who suffer.

Natural Teachable Moments

- When your child feels that she is not accepted by the "in" crowd
- Before or after your family relocates
- When your child is discriminated against because of her personality, abilities, ethnicity, or faith

AT SOME POINT, EVERY PERSON EXPERIENCES what it is like to live in exile. Exile can be exclusion from the "in" crowd at school, lack of appreciation at work, or a sense of disconnection from your family. The Jewish people in the Old Testament knew what it was like to be in exile. In 587 BC the Babylonians destroyed their great city of Jerusalem, including their beautiful temple, where they worshipped God. They were forcibly brought from their homes in Judah to the foreign culture of Babylon. They had to make new lives in a strange land. They were severely mistreated by the Babylonians, and they mourned for friends and family who had been killed during the war.

It was a very difficult time—but it was also a time for understanding the mercy of God. God sent the Jews a prophet whose words, "Give comfort to my people," are written in Isaiah 40:1. These words today are full of hope, as they were when the prophet proclaimed them to the people. God never abandons anyone and is a constant source of comfort and relief. We always have hope because God brings good and often surprising things out of bad circumstances.

Starting the Conversation

Recall with your child some times in your life or the life of your family when you turned to God for hope and comfort. Discuss any special prayer, tradition, or ceremony that helped in your time of need.

To Help You Connect

When sharing a personal experience or story with your child, be sure to invite her to ask questions about it. Tell her not only what happened but also how you felt and perceived the situation, as well as how you chose to respond. Draw out for your child how your beliefs affected your response—or how your faith would change your response if that same experience were to happen today.

TO SUPPORT YOU

SUGGESTED BIBLE READING
God comforts the Jews in exile: Isaiah 40:1–2

WHAT THE CHURCH SAYS ABOUT THIS TOPIC
During the reigns of King David and King Solomon, Israel was as powerful as any territory in the region. After the death of Solomon, however, Israel split into two kingdoms, and the neighboring territories of Babylon and Assyria grew stronger; the Israelites faced doom. The prophets and the authors of the historical books of the Old Testament interpreted the subsequent exile of the Jewish people as God's punishment for the people's worshiping God but ignoring the needs of the poor and needy.

The exile had a devastating impact on the Israelites, for they had lost much of what they felt tied them to God: their land, their temple, and their independence as a nation. The book of Lamentations gives expression to the pain they felt. Even though the exile was traumatic for the Israelites, God helped them draw good out of evil: under the pressure of that time they began the process of gathering their sacred writings, which Christians call the Old Testament.

A Prayer Moment with Your Child
Let's ask God to give us the strength we need during difficult times:
God, our Father, thank you for fulfilling what the prophets say
and giving people comfort and hope.
When I am hurt and alone,
please help me feel your constant love and presence.
Amen

32

Making memories

Faith Themes

In celebrating the Mass, we remember what Jesus has done for us.
At the Last Supper, Jesus gave us a way to remember him.

Natural Teachable Moments:

- On a rainy Sunday afternoon when your child has already spent time in front of the TV, computer, or video games
- After teaching your child how to cook a particular dish that you gather to eat together
- When putting together a family album or collage

A MOTHER ASKED HER GROWN DAUGHTERS what some of the happiest memories from their childhood were. Both of them enthusiastically replied that their happiest memories were from the times the family went camping. They treasured watching their mother create a little piece of home around the tent and picnic table at the campsite. They enjoyed having no phones or TV sets and leaving the daily concerns of life behind for a few days. And they prized the long evening hours spent sitting around the campfire listening to family stories and tall tales. Memories such as these are the glue that bind a family and make it strong. These memories depend on feelings of togetherness, not on money or material goods. What memories are you creating for your child today?

Starting the Conversation

Ask your child about his favorite memory of something your family did. What makes it so special and memorable? Share your favorite family memory as well.

To Help You Connect

You may want to share with your child a story about a special nonholiday meal that you have had with your family, such as a wedding, an anniversary, or a family reunion. Try to include details such as sights, sounds, and smells. Explain what made this memory so special to you. Special meals play an important role in banding a family together and strengthening its identity. They also play an important role in the Catholic faith. It may be helpful to your child if you point out this similarity.

TO SUPPORT YOU

SUGGESTED BIBLE READING
The institution of the **Eucharist** at the **Last Supper** is remembered: Luke 22:14–20

WHAT THE CHURCH SAYS ABOUT THIS TOPIC
Just as a family remembers and celebrates important family memories, there are many special events that Catholics remember and celebrate in the faith. The most fundamental of these we remember when we celebrate **Mass.** During Mass, Catholics take part in a memorial of the Last Supper, the meal that Jesus ate with his disciples the night before he died. He broke bread that night and gave it to his disciples along with a cup of wine, telling them it was his body and blood and charging them to partake in the meal in memory of him. We continue every day, especially on Sunday, to memorialize the Last Supper in our celebration of Mass.

When we celebrate Mass, we anticipate the heavenly banquet in the **kingdom of heaven.** Jesus said that God's kingdom was like a banquet at which we will sit at the table and dine with our heavenly Father.

In the Bible, meals are much more than a means to satisfy physical needs. The Hebrew people viewed sharing a meal as a way of expressing and strengthening relationships with one another under God's **covenant.** For example, in eating with outcasts, Jesus formed relationships with them and brought them into the family circle. It is no coincidence that, in the Gospel stories, meals are often the setting of Jesus' teachings and miracles.

At Mass, we bring to the table of the Lord all the love and joy that we have experienced in sharing meals with our family at home. In return we receive the Body and Blood of Christ as our food for the journey. The meals we share both at home and at church bring life and meaning to us.

A Prayer Moment with Your Child

Let's thank Jesus for the Last Supper, which we specially remember at Mass, and for all the other wonderful memories we have to celebrate:

Thank you, Jesus, for giving yourself to me.
And thank you for my family and friends,
with whom I have made wonderful memories.
Amen

33

Developing the skill to listen

Faith Themes

Prayer is a relationship with God, and there are many different ways to pray. When we pray, we are listening to and talking with God.

Natural Teachable Moments

- When tucking in your child at bedtime
- When you walk with your child: accompanying her to school, strolling through the neighborhood after a meal, hiking through a park or along a beach
- When your child interrupts your personal prayer or quiet reflection time

IN THE BIBLE, THE PROPHET ELIJAH, hiding in a cave from his enemies, wondered where God was in his life. God spoke to Elijah and told him to go outside the cave because God would be passing by. Just then, a great, strong wind came, followed by an earthquake, and then a fire. Elijah, however, could not find God in any of these. Soon after came a tiny whispering sound, and it was through this quiet sound that Elijah really heard God. This story teaches us a profound truth: God is always speaking to us, but we have to quiet down to hear God. Through silence our prayers move beyond words to heart-to-heart conversations with God. As we help our children learn to pray, we can also be examples of listening love.

Starting the Conversation

Amid all the family's obligations and activities, when can your family find quiet time? Talk with your child about the importance of quiet time and of settling down and listening to God. Discuss when would be a good time and place in your family routine for "God time."

To Help You Pray

At some point during prayer time with your child, take a moment beforehand to explain the reason behind two things that Christians commonly do when praying: folding hands and saying "Amen." Explain that, although we can pray in any position, there is a special way to use our hands when we pray that shows our respect to God. We fold our hands during prayer—with our palms closed and together, usually in front of our hearts, and our fingers extended and pointing upward. Folding our hands like this is a sign that we are putting our hearts and hands at the service of God, who loves us. Explain that prayer without folding hands is not "wrong" and is still prayer. Folding our hands is just a special thing we do, when we are able. You then might also explain that *Amen* is a word that means: "This is true." It's a reverent way of saying, "Yes, I agree." We speak this as the last word of any prayer to show that we really mean the words we have just said.

TO SUPPORT YOU

SUGGESTED BIBLE READING
Listening to God leads us to Jesus: John 6:45

WHAT THE CHURCH SAYS ABOUT THIS TOPIC

Public prayer is prayer that we offer in community with others. In our public prayers (such as **Mass,** the **sacraments,** and the Liturgy of the Hours), we talk to God in word and song and hear his word proclaimed to us in the Scriptures and in homilies. The reading, speaking, and singing are part of the prayerful experience.

Private prayer is prayer that we offer alone. In much of our private prayer (such as morning and evening prayers, **blessings** before and after meals, and reciting the rosary), we talk to God and express our thoughts and sentiments. As in public prayer, the words are part of the prayerful experience, and they can help us stay focused on God. The church also has an ancient tradition of wordless prayer—**contemplation**—in which a person rests in the presence of God and makes no attempt to use words to communicate with God. In one form of prayer, called **Lectio Divina,** the person praying uses the words of Scripture as a springboard to achieve quiet contemplation.

In every form of prayer, there should always be an element of listening so that God can communicate his love to us.

A Prayer Moment with Your Child

Let's ask God to help us listen in prayer:
Dear God, help me be still and to listen when I pray.
You are everywhere and will always be with me whenever I pray.
Help me be quiet and hear you in my heart.
Amen

34

Practicing small acts of kindness

Faith Themes

All life is sacred.
Small acts of social justice make a big difference.

Natural Teachable Moments:

- When your child tells you about a social injustice or environmental problem discussed in school
- When your child sees informational ads, commercials, or documentaries about starving children, wars, environmental neglect, and so on
- When your parish collects food for a community pantry or a holiday meal

FREDERIC OZANAM (1813–1853) WAS A CATHOLIC LAYMAN IN FRANCE. In 1832 an epidemic of cholera swept through Paris, killing up to 1,200 people each day. As Frederic walked through the poorer suburbs on his way to the university where he was a student, he was deeply moved at the hopeless state of families who had lost fathers and mothers. He and his six friends decided to see what they could do. They began by giving a widow the remainder of their winter wood supply. Frederic and his friends continued their work, and soon they were helping the less-fortunate people of Paris in many ways. Some people scoffed and asked, "How can seven men make a difference?" But they did. Eventually they formed an association and called it the **Society of St. Vincent de Paul.** The society they began has today some 107,000 members in the United States and 1,000,000 worldwide in 130 countries, providing aid in the form of medical supplies, food for the poor, counseling and education programs, and other services.

As Christians, we are called to care for one another and for the world God created through small acts that are part of our daily lifestyle. We don't have to look very far to find where we're needed; if we pay attention, the opportunities are usually right under our noses, in our own families, schools, parishes, and neighborhoods. As **Mother Teresa** once said, "We can do no great things— only small things with great love."

Starting the Conversation

Share with your child the story of Blessed Frederic Ozanam or another person whose life shows that small acts of kindness can make a big difference. Explain how the person did not listen to those who doubted that his or her efforts could make a difference, but took action to respond to a need right there at that time. Discuss what your child can do this month to show respect for human life.

To Help You Connect

Your child's world is growing. He is becoming more aware of peers, school and parish communities, and the wider world of the human race. There are several **Catholic social teaching** themes that can serve his growing consciousness. One is "Life and Dignity of the Human Person," which teaches us that all life is sacred and that all people must be treated with dignity and respect. Catholic social teaching, founded on the primacy of the human person's inherent worth and dignity, stresses a commitment to the common good. You may want to share with your child examples from your personal experience of how serving God's creation sustains human life, the environment, and the human community. Did you ever play peacemaker between two people or groups who were fighting? Did you ever volunteer to help refugees or victims of a natural disaster? Do you recycle? Developing your child's awareness of this will eventually disclose to him the face of the living God in himself, in other people, and in whole communities.

TO SUPPORT YOU

SUGGESTED BIBLE READING

Everyone who loves is of God and knows God: 1 John 4:7

WHAT THE CHURCH SAYS ABOUT THIS TOPIC

Human life has always been regarded as sacred in the Catholic tradition. One reason we hold the dignity of the human person in such high esteem is that we place value on human life, associating death with sin and associating life with all that is good and beautiful. Human life is the highest form of life on earth because it is directed toward eternal life. The church defends human life against all its enemies: killers associated with abortion, euthanasia, murder, and war, as well as slow killers such as poverty, hunger, discrimination, oppression, and homelessness.

Human life is part of the web of life, and Catholics believe that all life is sacred. There is interdependence among all life forms, so it is not possible to protest and defend human life while neglecting or irresponsibly using or taking advantage of animal and plant life. We are part of an ecological network of life with its origins in the Divine Life, and God's creation cannot be mistreated without showing disrespect for the creator.

A Prayer Moment with Your Child

Let's pray and thank Jesus for helping us treat every person and all of God's creation as sacred:

Jesus, thank you for showing me how to respect the world

and the people and creatures in it.

Help me always to live in peace with others.

Amen

35

Handling bullies and other enemies

Faith Themes

Jesus challenges us to love our enemies.

The fourth through tenth commandments teach us how to live in right relationship with others.

Natural Teachable Moments

- When you learn that a school bully or neighborhood gang is harassing your child, and after you have taken any necessary safety precautions or disciplinary action
- When another child or team is being overly competitive about a sporting event or regularly played game, such as a neighborhood baseball or a video game
- When your child is teased, excluded, or lied to

THOMAS MORE (1478–1535) WAS AN ENGLISH LAWYER devoted to his family. His story has long captured our popular imagination; his life was the basis of the famous play and Hollywood movie *A Man for All Seasons*. Thomas was a wonderful father to his three daughters and one son. He insisted that his daughters be educated and learn to read, something not usually done at that time. He became lord chancellor of England, a very powerful political position, and served King Henry VIII, whom Thomas had befriended and tutored.

After some years of success in his public career, Thomas was asked by the Catholic king Henry to approve the king's divorce so that he could marry another woman. Thomas, a faithful Catholic, refused and lost his position. Then when Henry declared himself the head of the church in England—effectively dismissing the authority of the pope in Rome—Thomas again objected and this time was imprisoned. When Thomas resisted all attempts to change his mind, he was finally executed. Throughout his ordeal, he followed Jesus' command to love his enemies, and he continued to love Henry VIII. On the day Thomas died, he told the crowd who witnessed his execution that he died "the king's good servant, but God's first." Thomas More was made a saint in 1935; his feast day is June 22.

Jesus told us that it is easy to love the people who are good to us—even hard-hearted people can do that—but we are called to forgive and to love our *enemies.* Jesus wants us not to fight aggression with aggression, but instead to love people who are unkind and to pray for them. Loving our enemies in daily life is not easy, but it brings us close to God and God's kingdom. It is one way to show that we love and serve God above all else.

Starting the Conversation

Ask your child who she might consider her enemy and why. Suggest that she forgive this person (or persons) and, remembering that all people are children of God, pray for this person.

To Help You Pray

The call to love one's enemy is one of the most challenging spiritual truths that Jesus taught. It requires that we take the personal mindset of having "no enemy" and instead loving *everyone.* A good place to begin exploring this concept with your child is in prayer. When you pray with her, try asking her to bring to mind the image of the person or group who is bullying, teasing, discriminating against, judging, lying to, threatening, or otherwise hurting her. Then have her say that person's name as reverently as possible in the sentence, "_____ is a child of God." As you continue to pray, ask your child to imagine what life is like for this person. Is this person insecure? Imprisoned by hate and fear? Dependent on a substance? Suffering from disorders? Have your child pray, "**Holy Spirit,** help me love _____."

This simple practice is a first step toward starting a healing process in your child's heart. When she is sincerely ready, add a final step: say a loving prayer with her for this person's soul and well-being here on earth. If there is a specific temptation or behavior that is plaguing the person, pray for him or her to be free of it. With this prayer practice your child begins a journey to peacemaking and develops the ability to live Jesus' command to "love your enemies."

TO SUPPORT YOU

SUGGESTED BIBLE READING
Jesus explains the **Ten Commandments** and teaches us about loving our enemies: Matthew 5:17–48

WHAT THE CHURCH SAYS ABOUT THIS TOPIC
While the first through third of the Ten Commandments teach us how to love God above all else, the fourth through tenth show us how to live in good relationship with others and society. Though the commandments are authoritative, they need to be interpreted in context. For example, the commandment not to steal has enduring merit, but the church has long maintained the notion that if a person is in extreme, life-threatening necessity, he or she "has the right to take from the riches of others what he himself needs." The commandment to obey lawful authority, such as our parents, always remains valid, although we must disobey immoral laws and orders.

The fifth commandment, which tells us not to kill, remains in essence valid, but this does not deny the right to defense as a means to render an immediate and unjust aggressor unable to inflict harm. Since love toward oneself is a fundamental principle of God's moral order, someone who defends his or her life is not guilty of murder if forced to mortally wound an unjust aggressor. However, the attack must be of the present moment, without hate or anger, and the goal should always be not to cause harm but to render the aggressor unable to cause harm. This is a loving response, as the unjust attack would wound not only oneself physically but also the aggressor's own soul spiritually. Such legitimate self-defense is a grave duty for those responsible for the lives of others and the common good.

A Prayer Moment with Your Child

It can be very hard to follow Jesus' teaching to love our enemies; let's thank the Holy Spirit in prayer for giving us the strength and understanding to do this:

Holy Spirit, thank you for giving me the strength to keep God's commandments.

I want to love all people, including those who hurt me and are not being friendly.

Help me always to trust that love is the best way to be at peace with others.

Amen

36

Celebrating Sunday Mass

Faith Themes

Jesus' community is the church.
Jesus calls us to share his love with others.

Natural Teachable Moments

- During a Friday or Saturday family meal in preparation for Sunday Mass
- When one of your children is preparing for first communion
- During your child's birthday party

YOU ARE KNEELING QUIETLY DURING **MASS** ON SUNDAY. People are still receiving Holy Communion. After your personal prayer, you take a little time to reflect on your fellow parishioners. A large family passes by, the children lively and restless. A retired religious sister returns to her place, her walker clicking on the floor. A young twentysomething couple displays the energy and interest of career seekers just out of college. You notice them all: young, elderly, men, women, some with a sparkle in their eyes, some with "Why am I here?" looks on their faces. God calls everyone. Each one of us has something extraordinary to offer. Every single person has gifts, talents, spirit, experiences—something special to share. What unique gifts do you bring to God's community?

Starting the Conversation

Your child also brings a unique gift to God's community. Explore with him what that gift is. What does he excel at, enjoy, have a natural ability for, or aspire to? Some way exists for your child to contribute positively to the community by using this gift. Help him identify various possibilities.

To Help You Connect

There are many ways to show your child his own gifts and how these might be applied in his school or parish community. Suppose he is a good reader. After reading aloud together, you might say, "Honey, you read that beautifully. Have you ever considered being a church lector someday?" Or perhaps you have a very active child with lots of energy. You might say, "You're big and strong, and like to get things moving. You'd make a good helper at the local nursing home, where they need lively kids like you on Sundays to wheel Catholic patients in wheelchairs down the corridors to the chapel for Mass. Do you feel like 'driving'?" Or you might say to your outgoing child, "I noticed that you welcomed our new neighbor, Bobby, just wonderfully and introduced him to other girls and boys on our street. In our faith we call that 'hospitality.' I think you have a real gift for hospitality. Maybe you'd like to be part of our parish's special welcoming committee that greets new families?"

TO SUPPORT YOU

SUGGESTED BIBLE READING

The early Christians demonstrate deep love for God and for one another:
Acts 2:42–47

WHAT THE CHURCH SAYS ABOUT THIS TOPIC

When we share with others, we give them something that is ours. Jesus' message is all about giving. He taught us that his Father had given his only Son to us for our salvation. Jesus himself gave his life for us so that we might live. Having ascended into heaven, he gives us the Holy Spirit so that our hearts will be filled with the love of God. Through the Spirit, we are called to give of ourselves to others, and when we do so with free hearts, we are filled more and more with God's love.

Sharing with others is a goal toward which the church constantly urges us. Catholics pray in the words of the late **Pope John Paul II:** "May rich and poor recognize that they are brothers and sisters; may they share what they have with one another as children of the one God who loves everyone, who wills the good of everyone, and who offers to everyone the gift of peace!" The sharing that the church has in mind is more than just financial; we are challenged to share with others our love, our faith, our presence, and our commitment to work for integrity and peace.

For example, when we share the **sign of peace** at Mass by shaking hands or embracing our family, friends, and neighbors, we acknowledge our reconciliation with God and with one another. We also state that, as a Christian community, we are committed to work for peace in the world. When we go to communion, then, we approach the table of the Lord as a reconciled people dedicated to peace.

A Prayer Moment with Your Child

Let's pray now and thank Jesus for teaching us how to act in our community and our parish:

Jesus, my friend and teacher, thank you for showing me that,
when sharing with others the special things I can do and give,
I show my love for you and other people.
Amen

37

Suffering when it can't be avoided

Faith Themes

We can reach out to others who are suffering.
Jesus redeemed us from our sins through his life, death, and resurrection.

Natural Teachable Moments

- When your child or someone she loves gets sick or is stricken with a serious illness
- When your child begins to learn about death
- When your child has a crush on someone who will not return her affections

A CHILD BROUGHT HOME A BABY BIRD THAT HAD FALLEN FROM ITS NEST. From the shape of the wing, it was obvious to the child's parents that the wing was badly broken. The bird would not survive. The child cried, and there was little the parents could do but share the pain. We would like to create a place for our children in which suffering could be avoided. But death and physical and emotional pain are a part of every life.

How can we find meaning in the midst of suffering? We find the answers in our relationship with God. In the midst of his suffering on the cross, Jesus reached out to the thief being crucified next to him. With the help of the **Holy Spirit,** we can reach out to others when we suffer and let others reach out to us. And when we encounter others who are in pain, we can be present to them and share in their suffering. In sharing the pain of our children, we help them learn to share the pain of others.

Starting the Conversation

Ask your child what suffering she has witnessed this week—someone who fell, a neighbor who lost his job, a child rejected by her playmates? Remind your child that suffering is an unavoidable part of the world. Jesus came so that he could be our companion in life, especially when we suffer. We can also be companions to those who are suffering through our prayers, words, and actions. Discuss how your child can respond to the suffering that she sees daily.

To Help You Listen

Many children will have no difficulty providing an example of suffering they have seen in their world. However, if your child has a difficult time coming up with an example of another person's suffering, this may mean she is reluctant to answer or is having trouble empathizing with others. If either is the case, check the news and current events; look for things that are part of the national conversation of the day. Share these with your child and let her see how the lesson of caring about others' suffering ties into everyday life and news. The news provides *lots* of examples of the pain of this world that you can use to teach your child how to care for others, especially at a local level. Or perhaps you can share a good news story about someone who has responded positively to a problem in the world and made a difference.

TO SUPPORT YOU

SUGGESTED BIBLE READING

Jesus promises salvation to a criminal who was being crucified with him:
Luke 23:39–43

WHAT THE CHURCH SAYS ABOUT THIS TOPIC

Throughout the Gospel of Luke, concern for people who are poor, suffering, or vulnerable is evident. Jesus is born in a stable and is visited not by kings, but by poor shepherds. When his parents take him to the temple to offer him to God, they bring two doves, the typical offering made by poor people.

Luke's Gospel tells us how Jesus shows special concern for the poor and suffering; for example, in the parable of the **Good Samaritan** he praises the rejected outsider who stops to aid the suffering man abandoned by others. Likewise, it is not surprising to find Jesus dying between two criminals. Jesus shares his death as well as his life with the poor, suffering, and the vulnerable.

Through his death on the cross, Jesus saved us from our sins. Although buried after his death, Jesus did not remain in the tomb, but rose from the dead, appearing numerous times to his disciples before ascending into **heaven.** Because Jesus' life, death, and resurrection redeemed us from sin—a human condition that began with humanity's break with God, told in the story of **Adam and Eve**—we can now stand in right relationship with God. This means that we receive God's gracious forgiveness, as well as the capacity to respond out of love to God's invitation and to others' suffering.

A Prayer Moment with Your Child

Let's take a few moments to pray and thank Jesus for being our savior and bringing peace to all who suffer:

Loving Jesus, you teach me how to be aware of the needs of others.
Thank you for saving me from my sins
through your life, death, and resurrection,
and help me to help others who are in pain.
Amen

38

Seeing prejudice for what it is

Faith Themes

All people are children of God.
Through his words and deeds, Jesus showed us how to love others.

Natural Teachable Moments

- When you observe your child exhibiting a prejudice, especially the subtle kind revealed in casual speech
- When your child is the subject of, or contributes to, discrimination
- When your child witnesses you or your spouse being prejudicial toward a person or group of people

JESUS FACED THE ISSUE OF DEEP PREJUDICE when he told the story of the **Good Samaritan**. The people of his time had been taught as children not to associate with Samaritans, who were considered unworthy. In telling the Good Samaritan parable—in which a Samaritan man helps an injured and abandoned Jewish stranger—Jesus was attacking such prejudices. Our children absorb our prejudices every day—in the stories we tell, in the way we interact with others in public, in what we don't do or say, in the way we treat their friends. It is important to remember that Jesus calls us to treat all people as children of God.

Starting the Conversation

Discuss with your child ways he can treat others fairly. Are there prejudicial attitudes that your child experiences at home or school that you want to talk about and address with him?

To Help You Listen

Since as much as two-thirds of all effective communication is nonverbal, make sure your body language communicates your enthusiasm for listening to and sharing with your child. For example, before you begin, relax your entire body; you don't want to communicate tension or conflict. Also, our faces, more than any other body part, reveal emotions, opinions, and moods, so it is important for you to maintain a facial expression that shows how wholeheartedly you care about your child's inner life and his relationship with God. Be aware of how your facial expressions communicate your feelings about your child's responses. Likewise, voices are just as unique as faces. You can develop vocal habits that can be helpful when sharing with your child, such as speaking clearly and slowly enough to be understood without sounding forced. Speak with confidence and enthusiasm to engage and inspire. And, as much you possibly can, speak from your heart.

TO SUPPORT YOU

SUGGESTED BIBLE READING
Jesus teaches about mercy and love by telling a parable: Luke 10:25–37

WHAT THE CHURCH SAYS ABOUT THIS TOPIC
The Good Samaritan story is a model for loving one's neighbor. The Samaritans were a group of people who lived in Israel at the time of the New Testament.

They were the descendants of the people left behind when many of the Jewish people were exiled to Babylon in 587 BC. They intermarried with non-Israelites who were brought into the country by the Assyrians. After 536 BC, when the exile of the Jewish people ended and the Jewish nation was restored, the Samaritans were not welcomed back into the Jewish community. The Jews in Jesus' time looked down upon the Samaritans as not being true followers of the Jewish religion. The Samaritans thought otherwise.

In telling the story of the Good Samaritan, Jesus was confronting his listeners with their own prejudices and emphasizing the unconditional, universal nature of God's love. In the story, a priest and then a Levite do not stop to help an injured man on the side of the road, but instead pass by him. The priests and the Levites (a member of the Hebrew tribe of Levi, one of the twelve tribes of Israel) were Israel's spiritual leaders at the time; in the story they represent the accepted teachings of the Jewish people. They are examples of law-observing people who did not aid the injured man because they were afraid of becoming defiled and unable to fulfill their religious duties. The question Jesus is posing here is, What is a religious person's true duty to God and to others?

A Prayer Moment with Your Child

We talked about ways we can try to be more like Jesus. Let's thank Jesus for showing us how to treat others and ask for his help as we continue to try to be kind and loving to all people:

Jesus, my friend, thank you for being my example and guide.
Help me be a Good Samaritan to others.
Amen

39

Nurturing your child's gifts and talents

Faith Themes

Jesus sees possibilities in Peter, and in all of us.
Jesus invites his followers to enter the kingdom of God.

Natural Teachable Moments

- When your child watches a movie, TV show, or news program about a prodigy or a person with exceptional abilities
- When your child enjoys, and excels in, a subject, hobby, or sport
- When an internal trait or mark of character in your child stands out

WHEN JESUS CALLED **PETER** TO BE HIS DISCIPLE, Peter asked Jesus to leave, feeling unworthy. Peter did not see the possibilities in himself that Jesus did. Peter was an intelligent man with an established trade. He did not want to think beyond day-to-day concerns, but Jesus recognized Peter's talents and called him to become the leader of the church. As parents we have the best opportunity to recognize and nurture the talents of our children. Many parents are tempted to see possibilities that do not suit a child's personality or abilities. By recognizing and nurturing each child's true talents and abilities, we can help our children become who God is calling them to be.

Starting the Conversation

Tell your child some of your dreams. Ask her, "What do you want to be when you grow up? Why?" Listen to her dreams and encourage the development of her talents.

To Help You Listen

When your child is sharing her dreams with you, listen closely and try to discern the deeper message behind her words. Did she say that she wants to be a cartoonist? Perhaps she has artistic and creative talents—or perhaps it is the adventurous spirit of her favorite cartoon character that prompts such a response. Did your child say she wants to be a banker like her cousin Mike? Perhaps she likes math and is good with numbers—or perhaps this dream is more about Mike's warm and generous personality that your child aspires to. To get at the deeper answers, you will likely have to ask her several times to explain her response. And however practical or impractical her dreams may be, try to offer some realistic hobby or activity that might help her, at this age, to explore her dreams.

TO SUPPORT YOU

SUGGESTED BIBLE READING
Jesus calls Peter to follow him, and Peter answers the call: Luke 5:1–11

WHAT THE CHURCH SAYS ABOUT THIS TOPIC
When Jesus gathered followers, he entrusted them with a special task: spreading the Good News of the **kingdom of God.** His followers formed the early church, headed by Peter. Christians have long reflected on the mission of the church.

Our contemporary understanding of this mission is reflected in the documents of the **Second Vatican Council.**

The council tells us that all Christians have been sent by Christ to reveal and communicate the love of God to all people and all nations. The goal is to bring all people to share in Christ's saving redemption. So that salvation may be proclaimed to the whole human race, we must bring the message of Christ to everyone—whether by words, actions, or simply by our way of being. Our mission is to shed the radiance of the gospel message on the whole world.

One way of summarizing this is to say that it is the mission of the church to proclaim the kingdom of God. The council then completes the picture by saying that it is the mission of the church to serve the kingdom of God everywhere—not for its own sake, but solely for the glory of God.

A Prayer Moment with Your Child

Now let's thank Jesus for his guidance in our lives and ask for his help in the future:

Dear Jesus, I want to trust you to guide my life as Peter did.
Thank you for calling me to follow you.
Help me to know and serve God.
Amen

40

Watching small things grow

Faith Themes

Small acts of kindness and love yield a great harvest.
The parable of the mustard seed teaches us about the kingdom of God.

Natural Teachable Moments

- When planting flowers, shrubs, or a garden with your child
- When your child measures his increasing height over time
- When your child observes or experiences a little act of kindness

OUR CHILDREN ARE FASCINATED WITH HOW AND WHY THINGS GROW. Either in schools or at home, they may have taken a small seed, planted it, watered it, and, with patience, watched it grow. Perhaps the plant had to be transplanted into a larger pot or into the ground to give its roots room to spread. From the tiniest beginnings, flourishing plants grow. It is no surprise that when Jesus spoke to his people, who were from an agricultural society, he used this image to describe the growth of the **kingdom of God**. In the same way, relationships within families are built on small acts of kindness and consideration. These small acts provide the foundation every family needs to grow together when facing the stresses of daily life.

Starting the Conversation

Share with your child what spending time with him and the whole family means to you. Recall a specific time when a small act of kindness or consideration within the family made all the difference to you. Explain how these small acts can have an effect far greater than the doer might expect, and ask if there are any little things your child might want to do for someone in your family or close circle this week.

To Help You Connect

If your child is shy about speaking to you from his heart—or thinks that such talk is strange or uncool—he is probably masking self-consciousness or a fear of being vulnerable. A good approach in this case is to model the behavior yourself by opening up first and sharing from your heart. Another tactic is to allow your child to witness you and your spouse or other family member engaged in meaningful, faith-filled conversation. Do this as regularly as possible. Also, it is important to create an unthreatening atmosphere in which to hold conversations about faith.

TO SUPPORT YOU

SUGGESTED BIBLE READING
The kingdom of God is compared to the tiny mustard seed that grows to be the largest of plants: Matthew 13:31–32

WHAT THE CHURCH SAYS ABOUT THIS TOPIC
Perhaps the predominant image in Jesus' preaching in the Gospels of Matthew, Mark, and Luke is the kingdom of God, also known as the **kingdom of heaven.** The concept of a kingdom was a familiar and natural one to the people of Jesus'

time, so it is not surprising that Jesus used that language to teach about God's authority and power. However, in the case of the kingdom of God, the emphasis is always on, not an area with geographical boundaries, but a *state of being* in which God actively rules. When God rules, the poor are vindicated, the oppressed liberated, and everyone experiences justice and peace.

In the book of Matthew, Jesus compared the growth of the kingdom of God to that of a tiny mustard seed. The mustard plant is an herb that begins as a very small seed but can grow up to six feet high and spread out over a large area.

The point of the **parable of the mustard seed** is to provide an accessible metaphor for the kingdom of God. The mustard seed is described as being small, almost invisible, but nonetheless effective because it grows to become a large bush and a haven for many of God's creatures.

Like the mustard seed, the scope and influence of the kingdom of God cannot be defined by size. The kingdom has no specific size because it is not a physical place. It is a state of being that is everywhere because of the love and strength of Jesus and his followers.

A Prayer Moment with Your Child

Jesus told us many stories about what it's like to live in God's love and rule. Let's become quiet now and thank Jesus for this:

Thank you, Jesus, for teaching me about the kingdom of God
and how great things can grow from something small
under your guidance.
Help me continue to grow in strength,
in understanding, in faith, and in love.
Amen

41

Caring for the environment

Faith Themes

Gospel of Life refers to an important document in the Catholic Church. All life is a sacred gift from God, and as God's people we have a special responsibility to care for the environment.

Natural Teachable Moments

- When your family recycles household materials
- When the media covers a story about damage to the environment
- When your child is with you in a grocery store where you are buying "green" products
- On Earth Day or during school events that show care for the environment

IN 1995 POPE JOHN PAUL II issued the encyclical *The Gospel of Life.* This document seeks to address the positive contribution of Catholic teaching regarding life in all its forms. Pope John Paul II noted that we have a specific responsibility toward the environment in which we live and toward the whole of creation that God has given to us. Our dominion of the earth is not an absolute power but must be based on God's dominion. This requires that we discern ways to serve the needs of this world rather than seek ways to exploit it for our own gain. Decisions that we make today not only will influence us but also will affect our children in the decades to come. What choices are we making today that demonstrate our care for the world and its creatures? In what ways are we being dismissive or irresponsible stewards of the world's resources and the life it supports?

Starting the Conversation

Ask your child what she would do to take responsibility and show care for the environment. Share one thing you did when you were her age or something that you'd like to do now. Try to pick one thing together that the two of you or your whole family could do for the environment sometime this month.

To Help You Ask Questions

Perhaps you can think together about the area that is within a mile radius of your home. Tell your child to imagine your home at the center of a circle a mile wide, and name places and things found within that area. Then ask if there is anything that can be done to help or improve this area. Are there any parks, streams, or alleys that need to be cleaned? Is there an unused piece of land that could be used as a community garden or planted with grass or native plants? Could you begin recycling something in your home that you currently are not? Can you walk or bike somewhere that you currently drive to? Try to find something that captures your child's imagination; avoid forcing her into an activity she might resent.

TO SUPPORT YOU

SUGGESTED BIBLE READING
God gives creation to humans, and creation rejoices:
Genesis 1:28–31 and Psalm 96:11–13

WHAT THE CHURCH SAYS ABOUT THIS TOPIC

A Catholic theology of the environment includes these principles:

God created everything that exists, and everything that God created is good. There is no such thing as a bad creation, and everything that exists must be respected as God given.

The world and all of its elements are "sacramental"—signs to us of God's power and wisdom and we use them to express our worship of God. This gives them added meaning as well as additional basis for respect.

Human beings are a part of, not apart from, the rest of creation. Our fate on earth is intimately linked to the well-being of the environment. We cannot take the position of outsiders looking in on the environment; rather, we must consider whatever happens to the environment as happening to us.

Human beings differ from the rest of God's creation because they are created with intellect and **free will,** which means that we are responsible for protecting the well-being of the environment. This responsibility exists on the personal level, obliging each one of us to be caring and protective in our use of natural resources. It also exists on the social level, obliging us as a society to make political and economic decisions that will not harm but enhance the environment.

Human beings have basic rights, but so do animals, plants, and the natural elements: land, water, and air. We cannot do as we please with the environment.

A Prayer Moment with Your Child

God has given us so many beautiful places and creatures to care for. Let's give him our thanks for this gift:

Creator God, thank you for the marvelous world you've made.
Show me how to care for it with love and wisdom,
now and for the future.
Amen

42

Answering the call to serve others

Faith Themes

We are to love as God loves.
Each one of us is called to be holy.

Natural Teachable Moments

- When someone in your family does volunteer work
- When your child shows clear concern for a societal problem or a person who is in need
- When your family is discussing the occupational choices of friends, neighbors, parishioners, or other members of society

WHEN **MOTHER TERESA** WAS LABORING FOR THE POOR, a reporter asked her what she thought about being called a saint. She replied that we are all called to be saints. She was called to be a saint in what she did, and the reporters, camerapersons, and producers were called to be saints in what they did. This is the biblical understanding of what it means to be holy. A holy person is not always perfect; a holy person responds to God's call to love him and serve others. Holiness means saying yes to God's constant invitation to a deeper relationship with God in prayer, in church and the sacraments, and in our daily lives and relationships with others. It does not mean trying to become Mother Teresa or St. Dominic or St. Ignatius; nor does it mean being like some imagined model of a saint. It means being the best "you" that God created and is calling you to be. As parents we, too, are called to be holy. We respond to God's call by serving our family members and by showing them God's love.

Starting the Conversation

Recall with your child memorable people who have touched your lives. What made them special? How did they serve God and others?

To Help You Pray

We express our spirituality through our prayers and our actions. In his prayer life, your child forms a personal relationship with God. There are many ways to pray. When your child engages in reflective prayer, he uses thoughts, words, memory, and imagination to have prayerful conversation with God. When he spends time in silence with God, using his feelings and being aware of God's presence, he is involved in what Catholics call spiritual **contemplation.** After prayer, your child goes forth into the world to live as he believes and as the **Holy Spirit** guides him. Catholics call this spirituality in action. Serving others is the primary manifestation of spirituality in action. Before or after your prayer together, you may want to explain to your child the relationship between these two modes of spirituality: prayer and service to others.

TO SUPPORT YOU

SUGGESTED BIBLE READING

Jesus teaches us the **Great Commandment:** Matthew 22:37–38

WHAT THE CHURCH SAYS ABOUT THIS TOPIC

Moral life can be summed up in terms of love of God, self, and neighbor. During his public ministry, a man asked Jesus, "What is the greatest commandment?" The Jewish people of the time followed the **Ten Commandments** that God had given to Moses. Jesus replied that the greatest commandment was to love God with all your heart, soul, and mind, and to love your neighbor as yourself. Christians call this the Great Commandment.

The New Testament understanding of love is based on the Old Testament understanding of **covenant** love: God's steadfast love will never waiver. This love is without conditions. Similarly the Christian who listens for and cooperates with the Holy Spirit will not waiver in his or her love for God. This type of love involves commitment and action to reach a better personal relationship with God. It shows a true appreciation for how much God loves each of us as individuals, and it shows our own willingness to serve our neighbors.

A Prayer Moment with Your Child

Jesus taught us how to live so that we can be happy and blessed. He shared with us the Great Commandment, which shows us how to follow God and make good choices. Let's thank him for the special words he gave us:

Thank you, Jesus, for teaching us the Great Commandment.
Help me try to follow this every day.
Amen

43

Recognizing virtue in your child

Faith Themes

The Beatitudes describe the Christian way to live.
Jesus shows us how we can be truly happy and share happiness with others.

Natural Teachable Moments

- When your child does something good and kind
- When your child helps without being asked
- When your child is gentle and forgiving

AS PARENTS WE HAVE MANY OPPORTUNITIES TO PRACTICE THE **BEATITUDES,** found in Matthew 5:1–10. We are poor in spirit when we recognize that we are dependent on God for help. We mourn when we are saddened at the way people suffer in the world. We act with meekness when we are slow to anger and gentle with our children in difficult times. We practice mercy when we truly forgive them. We are pure of heart when we share with our children our commitment to promote justice in the world. We have many opportunities to be peacemakers in the way we love and restore harmony in our families and in our protection of the dignity of each person. The Beatitudes comprise the virtues that help us create a Christian family.

Starting the Conversation

Share with your child a time when you noticed something she did that exemplified living the Beatitudes, such as forgiving a friend or sharing with someone younger. Compliment your child on her good Christian behavior. Let her know that you noticed.

To Help You Connect

Identify your child's behavior as "Christian," not merely "good." Your doing this does not show disrespect to other religious traditions. Living the Beatitudes is what Christ taught us, and when we follow Christ's teaching, we are being Christians. The word *Christian* means "follower of Christ." Because humans sin, Christians do not always act in a Christian manner—the manner that Jesus taught. But when we do, we can truly call our actions Christian.

TO SUPPORT YOU

SUGGESTED BIBLE READING
Jesus shows us how to *be* through the Beatitudes: Matthew 5:1–10

WHAT THE CHURCH SAYS ABOUT THIS TOPIC
The Beatitudes are a proclamation, a recipe, and a promise. As a proclamation, they reveal how Jesus calls us to live. As a recipe, they describe specific ways we can function in order to be happy and to live a life that is pleasing to God. As a promise, the Beatitudes describe the final destination to which Jesus calls us.

Some words and phrases in the Beatitudes require further explanation. "Poor in spirit" refers to the recognition of our dependence on God, regardless of social status or abilities. Those who live in poverty are to be cared for; the rich are at risk if they neglect God and the poor. Those who "mourn" suffer when witnessing people's unjust treatment of one another. "The meek" are those who are humble and who are "slow to anger" and/or "gentle with others." Those who are "merciful" pardon the wrongs of others. "Purity of heart" is similar to justice and includes trust in and loyalty to God's commands. "Peacemakers" are those who love their neighbors as they love themselves and seek to promote the well-being of all people.

The Beatitudes are at the heart of Jesus' preaching. They fulfill the promises of the Old Testament and prepare us for the **kingdom of God.**

A Prayer Moment with Your Child

Let's take a few moments to be aware of Jesus in our hearts and to talk to him about our thoughts and feelings about the Beatitudes:

Jesus, thank you for showing me how to live as you lived
so that I may be truly happy and share my happiness with others.
Help me to be kind to someone else each day.
Amen

44

Celebrating Christmas well

Faith Themes

Jesus' birth teaches us about humility and finding God in unexpected places.

Natural Teachable Moments

- Before an Advent or Christmas family tradition, such as setting out an Advent wreath or decorating the Christmas tree
- When you and your child watch a Christmas special on TV or video
- When you share the story of your child's birth

THE COMMERCIAL HYPE SURROUNDING **CHRISTMAS** seems to come earlier and earlier every year. The sentimental music, competitive decorations, bombastic advertisements, and blatant consumerism leave us exhausted. Who can really celebrate anything in the middle of all the noise? The true story of Jesus' birth is quite simple: it tells us that when we look for God, we will find him in unexpected places. When God the Father sent Jesus, he chose a humble stable for the birthplace. For Jesus' parents, God chose **Mary and Joseph**—good, modest people who loved and cared for Jesus. He selected poor shepherds to be the first to learn about the coming of Christ. At its heart, the Christmas story calls us to focus on God's presence all around us and to examine what is truly important in our lives. We can prepare for Christmas with planned moments of reflection and peace.

Starting the Conversation

Begin a discussion about how you will celebrate the holiday season in your home. How will you remember the birth of Jesus? Ask your child for his suggestions.

To Help You Connect

Children do not all learn in the same way. Some children are visual learners, some are auditory learners, and some are kinesthetic learners. As you engage your child in discussing faith, you may decide to read stories or passages from the Bible. This is especially good for auditory learners. You can make Scripture come more alive for your child by dramatizing your reading to appeal to his imagination and senses. Give the various characters different voices and enhance your reading with sound effects. If your child is a visual learner, he can read along with you. Kinesthetic learners can act out the stories in skits or role-playing, or they can voice certain parts.

TO SUPPORT YOU

SUGGESTED BIBLE READING
The story of Christ's birth and Mary's reflection on these events:
Luke 2:4–14 and 19–20

WHAT THE CHURCH SAYS ABOUT THIS TOPIC
The Gospels provide us with two accounts of the birth of Jesus. The account in the book of Matthew shows Jesus being welcomed on earth by magi, or wise men, from the east. The book of Luke's account shows Jesus being welcomed on earth by shepherds. Both Gospels record the birth of Jesus as taking place in

very humble surroundings, far away from home. Matthew's story tells us that Mary and Joseph named their son Jesus, which means "God saves." Luke's story of the birth features a tiny baby, a simple family in a town that is not their own, and shepherds—all people who occupy the lowest rungs of the social ladder. It is a story about the vulnerable people of society, those who often suffer the most. It is clear from the circumstances of his birth and the social situation of his family that Jesus was identifying himself with the poor, weak, and vulnerable of the world. As the Catholic Church reminds us, it is most often the weak and unfortunate, the poor, the aged, the very young, minorities, and women who are victims of injustice. The story of the birth of Jesus is both a lesson in humility and a reminder of our Christian obligation to stand up for the rights of the most vulnerable in our society.

A Prayer Moment with Your Child

Let's thank God together for giving us his Son, Jesus, and for Christmastime, which helps us remember Jesus' birth:

Thank you, God, for sending us Jesus.
May we celebrate in our hearts the gift of his birth this year,
and every year, at Christmas.
Amen

45

Welcoming others into our lives

Faith Themes

We can welcome Jesus into our lives.
How two disciples welcomed Jesus.

Natural Teachable Moments

- When a relative, exchange student, or other person moves in with your family
- When you have a new neighbor or there's a new child in school
- When someone in your child's regular group of friends introduces a new person into the circle

A YOUNG BOY COULD NOT HELP BUT NOTICE THAT HIS FRIEND was never available to play on Sunday mornings. When he asked, he learned that his friend's family went to Sunday **Mass.** Intrigued, the boy asked his parents' permission to attend Mass with his friend's family. They agreed, and he began to attend Mass with the family regularly. He became attracted to the faith through the hospitality of his friend's family.

The biblical story in Luke of the two disciples walking on the road with Jesus after the Resurrection is also a story of hospitality. Though the disciples did not recognize the resurrected Jesus, at the end of their walk together, the disciples asked Jesus to dine with them. In doing so, they were welcoming him into their lives. As a result, during the meal they were given the gift of seeing and recognizing the risen Christ when he blessed and broke the bread. Today when we show others hospitality and welcome them into our lives, we are also welcoming Jesus.

Starting the Conversation

Discuss with your child ways in which your family can better welcome people into your lives. Explain that being a welcoming person is a mark of following Jesus, who loved and welcomed all people.

To Help You Ask Questions

You might ask your child about a time when someone made her feel welcome. How did the person do that? Or ask about a time or place where she did not feel welcome. What could she do to help others who find themselves in a similar situation? For example, an act of hospitality can be something as simple as greeting someone in a loving manner or saying good-bye when the person leaves. Remember that you teach your child a great deal about Christian hospitality just through the manner in which you express yourself to her each day when you greet her or say good-bye. You are her primary model for how to welcome others, and you have numerous ordinary opportunities every week to nonverbally teach this behavior.

TO SUPPORT YOU

SUGGESTED BIBLE READING

Jesus walks and dines with two disciples on the **road to Emmaus:** Luke 24:13–35

WHAT THE CHURCH SAYS ABOUT THIS TOPIC

Jesus knew well what it meant to be unwelcome: his parents were unwelcome at the inn in Bethlehem at the time of his birth, and he was himself unwelcome in his home country of Judea during the time of King Herod. Yet Jesus welcomed everyone into his presence during his public life. Against the objections of more "proper" society, he welcomed children, the sick, outcasts, and sinners. For example, he made himself welcome in the house of the notorious sinner **Zacchaeus,** and he accepted the welcoming invitation of the two befuddled disciples who were on the road to Emmaus (em ā'es).

The exact distance of this village from the city of Jerusalem is disputed; it could have been from one to seven miles away. The story of the road to Emmaus is a beautiful portrayal of the disciples' journey into faith after the death and resurrection of Jesus. The two disciples are walking away from Jerusalem, discouraged by the events that led to Jesus' recent death there. Jesus joins them on the walk and explains the Scriptures to them, which the disciples find intriguing. As evening approaches the three finally arrive at an inn, and the disciples invite Jesus to stay with them and rest a while, and he accepts. The unrecognizable Jesus was a stranger to the disciples, and the inn's services would have cost a fee, just like today, so their offer was an act of welcoming and hospitality. They only realize who Jesus is when, in the fullness of hospitality, he breaks bread with them over a meal.

A Prayer Moment with Your Child

Let's pray and tell Jesus how welcome he is in our life:
Loving Jesus, you are always welcome in my life.
Help me to welcome others.
Amen

46

Honoring parents and elders

Faith Themes

God has given our parents to us, and we are called to honor and obey them. Jesus obeyed his parents.

Natural Teachable Moments

- On the birthday of your child's grandparent
- After your child has questioned your authority as a parent or why he should have to follow your orders
- When your child sees another child misbehaving in public

IT IS TEMPTING TO INTERPRET THE COMMANDMENT that tells children to honor their parents as a call for instant obedience. In biblical times, honoring one's parents meant respecting them as sources of wisdom and making a commitment to care for them in their old age. We, as sons and daughters ourselves, are the most influential example of what it means to respect parents. Especially now, while our children are in their formative years, we teach them the fundamental attitudes they will act out in their behavior toward us as they get older.

Starting the Conversation

Share with your child your favorite memories of your parents, your child's grandparents. Discuss ways your family can make life easier and more enjoyable for older relatives.

To Help You Connect

This is probably a good time to remind your child that you were once a child, too, and that you had to respect and obey your parents—or if they are living, that you still honor them. You might tell your child that you know it's not easy to obey parents, but we must remember that parents have rules for us because they love us. They want us to grow into healthy, happy people. They have lived longer than children have and have grown to see the harmful effects of certain decisions and actions. Even still, it can be very difficult at times for young people to respect and be obedient to parents and elders. Let your child know that he can always ask for God's grace to help him obey and grow up happy and healthy.

TO SUPPORT YOU

SUGGESTED BIBLE READING
Mary and Joseph search for and find Jesus, who grows up obedient to his parents: Luke 2:41–51

WHAT THE CHURCH SAYS ABOUT THIS TOPIC
The Catholic theology of the family teaches that the family is good for a couple because it provides a stable setting within which the couple can enjoy and develop their love. The family is good for children because it provides a safe, secure environment for their development and education. The family is good for society because it is on the foundation of the family that all other social communities are built. The family is good for the church because it is within the family as **domestic church** that people have their most meaningful experiences of

God's love, and it is out of the domestic church that believers come together to form parishes, dioceses, and the universal church.

Parents have the right to all means necessary to maintain a family, and they have the right to be respected for all that they do within the family. Children have the right to all means necessary to grow up and mature. They have the right to be respected as full human beings.

Parents have the responsibility to be faithful to each other and to care for the well-being of the family. Children have the responsibility to respect and obey their parents, to cooperate with those who help them mature, and to contribute to the well-being of everyone else in the family.

A Prayer Moment with Your Child

Let's thank Jesus for giving us his example to follow of how we show our love for parents and for God:

Jesus, Son of God, thank you for teaching me to obey
and to care for my parents and grandparents.
Amen

47

Turning to God in times of tragedy

Faith Themes

Jesus calls us to eternal life with our Father in heaven.
The church recognizes corporal and spiritual works of mercy.

Natural Teachable Moments

- After the sudden death of a friend or family member
- When a natural disaster strikes a community or another country, leaving pain, destruction, famine, disease, orphans, or homelessness
- When political oppression, social injustice, or genocide create a refugee crisis

IN THE DAYS AFTER SEPTEMBER 11, 2001, churches, synagogues, and mosques were filled with people. Around the world candles were lit. Impromptu shrines were filled with flowers and prayer intentions. Prayers were offered for the dead and their suffering families. In tragic times our children naturally have questions about God and **heaven.** Treat their questions with respect. Be patient, knowing that you do not have all the answers. Pray with your children for all those caught up in tragedy.

Starting the Conversation

Think of concrete ways that you as a family can be a source of help and comfort for those who suffer, especially those faced with tragic situations.

To Help You Connect

One practical and easy first step after a tragedy has struck a community, group, or country—the floods in New Orleans, the famines in Africa, or the tsunami in Asia—is to check the website of organizations such as Catholic Charities, the Campaign for Human Development, Red Cross, Amnesty International, Jesuit Refugee Service, and Catholic Relief Services. Or perhaps you can get on their mailing list beforehand. These organizations often distribute information about various ways people can immediately help after a disaster, such as donations of urgently needed goods and services. Also, check with your local parish to see what it might be organizing. Then help your child to appreciate the many good things that people of faith are doing in the world and to see how she might become part of this effort.

TO SUPPORT YOU

SUGGESTED BIBLE READING

Jesus' parable of the Last Judgment tells us that we will be judged according to our faith and how we treat others: Matthew 25:31–46

WHAT THE CHURCH SAYS ABOUT THIS TOPIC

In Catholic Church teaching, the **corporal and spiritual works of mercy** are actions we can perform that extend God's mercy and compassion to those in need. In order to better understand this, it is helpful to clarify what we mean by *God's* mercy. At **Mass,** during the penitential rite, we pray, "Lord, have mercy!" Sometimes, when we think of the word *mercy,* we picture someone throwing himself on his knees before a cruel villain, pleading to be spared some punishment. This is not our understanding of God's mercy. We do not ask for God's mercy because we are afraid of incurring God's wrath as punishment for our sins. Rather, when we call on God to have mercy, we are calling on God in the only way we know him—as one who responds with infinite compassion to those in need. When we show mercy to others, we are responding as God responds: with compassion. Works of mercy are opportunities to extend God's compassion to those in need.

There are two kinds of works of mercy: corporal and spiritual. Corporal works of mercy are the kind of acts by which we help our neighbors with their everyday material and physical needs. These include things like feeding the hungry, finding a home for the homeless, clothing the naked, visiting the sick and those in prison, giving alms to the poor, and burying the dead. Spiritual works of mercy are the kind of acts through which we help our neighbors meet the needs that are emotional and spiritual, including instructing, advising, consoling, comforting, forgiving, and bearing wrongs with patience.

A Prayer Moment with Your Child

Let's pray now to God, the source of all love and compassion:
God of judgment and mercy, thank you for your love,
which continually calls me to come closer to you.
Help me to see you in all people I meet
and to recognize how to serve you by helping others,
especially those in need.
Amen

48

Receiving spiritual nourishment

Faith Themes

For Catholics, the Eucharist is the real presence of Christ.
Jesus' presence in the Mass and the Eucharist feeds our souls.

Natural Teachable Moments

- When a family member is experiencing burnout at work or school
- Before your family goes to Mass together on Sunday to start the week
- When someone in the family is very sick (or dying)

THE RELIGIOUS SISTER (NUN) TOLD HER BROTHER what her daily life was like. She lived in South America and ministered to people who were poor and aged. As the youngest, healthiest sister in her religious community, she was responsible for going out to beg for their supper. Their village was impoverished and lacked wealthy families that could make large donations to support the order's work, so she had to beg on a daily basis. Each day as she left the home where she worked, she knew that all there would be for the aged and the sisters to eat that evening was what she would bring back. One day it might be a sack of dried beans. Another day it might be some fruit or bread. Every day she prayed to God, "Give us this day our daily bread"—and she understood what those words meant. She said she could face each day only because she attended **Mass** each morning and received the bread of life in the **Eucharist.** This spiritual nourishment gave her the inner strength to do what she did. Jesus Christ fed her soul so that she could feed his people. Jesus awaits us, and our children as well, so that we may be fed for our journeys.

Starting the Conversation

Discuss with your child the need everyone has to be nourished spiritually as well as physically and, consequently, the need for the frequent reception of Jesus in the Eucharist.

To Help You Connect

It can be difficult to talk to your child about the soul and the difference between physical and spiritual nourishment; these are challenging concepts even for adults. One approach is to explain that the human person is made of body, mind, and soul, and each of those elements needs to be fed regularly. Your child is familiar with feeding his physical body. Remind him of examples of his favorite healthful foods and how good he feels after eating them. Your child also knows about feeding the mind; he does this when he goes to school and learns new things that exercise his brain. He can put a lot of junk into his mind and it will eventually become dull and lazy, or he can learn true and natural things, causing his mind to be sharp and alive. Explain that, in a similar way, everyone has a soul that needs regular feeding, but what the soul "eats" is spiritual in nature, not physical. True nourishment for our souls comes only from God. God's love is spiritual nourishment. You may give examples of how God feeds us, but the Catholic Church teaches that the best example is Jesus' **real presence** in the Eucharist.

TO SUPPORT YOU

SUGGESTED BIBLE READING

Jesus tells us he is the bread of life: John 6:47–58

WHAT THE CHURCH SAYS ABOUT THIS TOPIC

Jesus is present in the celebration of Mass in many ways. First, Jesus is present in the presiding priest, who acts in the name of Christ. Jesus is also present in the assembly gathered for worship. Jesus is present in the proclamation of the Word, for he himself is the Word of God made flesh. Finally, Jesus becomes present during the great eucharistic prayer as the bread and wine are transformed into his Body and Blood.

Jesus is really present in all these ways, but Catholics use the term *real presence* to refer to the sacramental presence of Jesus under the appearances of bread and wine. Jesus' presence is real, not merely figurative or symbolic. St. John asserts that Jesus is the bread of life, the true bread come down from heaven for the life of the world (John 6:48–51). And the church in the Council of Trent (AD 1545–64) declared that after the consecration of bread and wine Jesus Christ is truly, really, and substantially present. This presence of the person of Jesus Christ (God and man) is what feeds us spiritually when we receive Holy communion.

A Prayer Moment with Your Child

Let's quiet ourselves and become aware in our hearts of Jesus' presence, and let's pray together:

Jesus, thank you for giving me yourself in the Eucharist.
Thank you for feeding my soul with life
when I celebrate this sacrament.
Amen

49

Appreciating diversity

Faith Themes

Being one in Christ enables unity in diversity.
The church is one, expressed in many ways.

Natural Teachable Moments

- Before a family trip, or when your child is studying different countries and cultures
- When a family of a different ethnic group from yours moves into the neighborhood
- When your child complains about a sibling being "strange" or acting differently than others (when you know this behavior is simply the sibling's personality)

AMERICA HAS OFTEN BEEN CALLED THE MELTING POT for people of many ethnic origins. Perhaps the image of salad bowl is more fitting, as each distinct flavor adds to the flavor of the whole. The Catholic Church is also a community of diverse cultures. Along with the experience of the Roman Catholic Church, there are some twenty **Eastern Catholic** churches that celebrate the liturgy in languages such as Armenian, Coptic, Arabic, and Malay. In the Roman Catholic Church, diverse spiritualities are clustered around the mission of religious orders such as the Passionists, the Dominicans, and the Jesuits. All of these make up the church; the word *catholic* means universal.

We come from nations all over the world, from the smallest to the largest. Our many cultures are different from one another and are very different from the culture that Jesus lived in. The source of our diversity is the **Trinity,** who created the world in all its infinite diversity. We are also one, united in the faith that we share with one another and with all of God's people who have gone before us. The source of our unity is the Spirit of God, who holds us together in faith, hope, and love. In a similar manner, your family can be made of members with diverse personalities, temperaments, and gifts—but you are one family, united by your love and the sacramental presence of Jesus in your lives.

Starting the Conversation

Ask your child to share her observations of how each member of your family is unique in one way from all other members. Suggest that she name something other than physical attributes, such as being tall or seven years old. Explore together how each characteristic or gift she mentions serves the family in some way. Point out that just as diversity in the family is a good thing, it is a good thing in the world and in Jesus' church.

To Help You Connect

At this time in your child's life, she is being exposed to the wider world, through sources such as school, sports, the Internet, and the news. Now is a good time to teach her that diversity is not something to be feared but to be celebrated as an important aspect of God's will. One way to experience this as family in regard to faith is to show your child the diversity of the people who make up the living church. One Sunday attend together a service that reflects a Catholic tradition different from your own. It might be a **Mass** in an Eastern Catholic Church, such as a Ukrainian or Armenian church, or a liturgy in a different language, such as a Spanish Mass. The phone book or Internet should provide ample examples from which to choose. Afterward, explore together how the service shows both the diversity and the unity in the church. What was the same as in your regular service? What was different?

TO SUPPORT YOU

SUGGESTED BIBLE READING
Through the **Holy Spirit,** we are one body with many parts:
1 Corinthians 12:12–21

WHAT THE CHURCH SAYS ABOUT THIS TOPIC
The church is often referred to as the "Body of Christ" to show the unity of Jesus with the church and the unity among its individual members. We are all brothers and sisters in Christ. There are different roles for members in the church, described in three broad categories: the clergy (such as priests and bishops), the "religious" who live in a community and take vows of poverty, chastity, and obedience (such as the Franciscans, the Trappists, and the Carmelites), and the laity (all others, who are called to be witnesses in the world and foster gospel values in society). All of these roles are fundamentally equal in the eyes of God and of the church. No role is inherently more holy than another, because the role itself is not holy—the person fulfilling that role is.

There are also different churches within the one Catholic Church—from what is known as the Eastern Catholic tradition. In AD 1054 the Eastern and Western churches split over political and religious matters. The Eastern churches traditionally celebrated Mass in their local languages (instead of Latin, as was celebrated in the Western churches) and did not recognize the primacy of the pope in Rome, instead viewing the patriarch of Constantinople as the "first among equals." These churches are referred to as **Orthodox** (for example, Russian Orthodox). Orthodox churches are not to be confused with the twenty-one Eastern Catholic churches (for example, the Ukrainian Catholic Church) that are in communion with Rome and do recognize the authority of the pope in Rome. While this diversity within the one Catholic Church can appear confusing at first, it is a reflection of the mystery of the Trinity: just as God is three persons, yet one God, so the Catholic Church is twenty-two unique church traditions, yet one church.

A Prayer Moment with Your Child

Let's pray now to Jesus, thanking him for his gift of unity in the church:

Jesus, thank you for making me a member of your church
and a part of a community that unites people from many places and times.
Help me accept and appreciate all the members of your family.
Amen

50

Respecting the power of words

Faith Themes

A moral life commits us to truth in our words and deeds.
Jesus helps us act responsibly toward others and with respect.

Natural Teachable Moments

- After you or your spouse has just apologized for making a harsh criticism
- When your child has damaged property in the house, whether intentionally, through horseplay, or by accident
- During the family meal

IN CHAPTER 3 OF HIS BIBLICAL LETTER, James describes the damage that can be done by an undisciplined tongue. James calls the tongue "a restless evil, full of poison" that no one can tame. Just as a spark can set a forest ablaze, an uncontrolled tongue can create a forest fire of damage in our human relationships. It is important to reflect on James's words when considering our role as parents. Does criticism of our children come more easily than praise? Do we find ourselves quicker to critique a child's accomplishments than to build his self-esteem? James calls us to gain the wisdom that comes from God so that our words will be "peaceable, gentle, compliant, full of mercy."

Starting the Conversation

Talk with your child about the effect on others of sincere compliments, praise, and kind words. As a family, make an effort to say one positive thing to one another every day this week.

To Help You Listen

Listening carefully to your child's use of words can be quite revealing. Does he tend to use words of encouragement, to give people the benefit of the doubt, and to point out the sunnier side of things? Commend him when he uses words in a gentle and heartening manner. Let your child know that in this way he is following Jesus' example. On the other hand, try not to judge and immediately correct your child when he speaks words of criticism—someone has cheap taste, or the world sucks, or his teacher is a blockhead. Though it may be unkind, it likely reflects his honest feelings and observations at the time.

Unless your child's words are so harsh or vulgar that they require immediate correction, simply suggest that his opinion may change if he remains open to the idea that change is possible. You may at times point out evidence contrary to your child's statement, but resist the urge to do this *every* time he makes a criticism, lest you create the perception that you always think his opinions are wrong.

TO SUPPORT YOU

SUGGESTED BIBLE READING

James cautions us to regulate our speech: James 3:1–12

WHAT THE CHURCH SAYS ABOUT THIS TOPIC

Words have power—ask any psychologist, poet, songwriter, or novelist. In biblical times great emphasis was placed upon the spoken word because most people could not read or write. The Hebrew people believed that when words were spoken, a dynamic energy was released that enabled the words to achieve what they signified. For example, in Genesis 27, **Jacob** deceived his father, **Isaac,** into granting him the blessing that was meant for **Esau,** the firstborn son. Isaac was unable to retract his blessing (Genesis 27:33) since the words had already been spoken. For this reason, oaths, promises, oral contracts, blessings, and curses were considered especially powerful. It is no wonder that two of the **Ten Commandments** regulate our use of words: we must not misuse God's name, and we must not lie. From the Gospels we learn that Jesus made a great impression on people because he delivered his words "with authority" (Mark 1:27).

Today, when someone says, "I give you my word," our response is an act of faith. If the person is true to his or her word, we are safe. If not, we are in trouble. God gave his word to the prophets with the knowledge that it would not come back to him empty. Throughout the Old Testament, God revealed himself to us through deed and word. In the New Testament, God gave us his Word, namely, his only son, Jesus Christ. The Gospel of John describes the incarnation of Jesus with this beautiful imagery: "and the Word became flesh and made his dwelling among us" (John 1:14). God's word as sacred promise is also known as a **covenant.** God is true to his word!

A Prayer Moment with Your Child

Let's meet Jesus in our hearts now and thank him for showing us how to use our words to bring peace and love into the world:

Jesus, thank you for showing me ways to use words for the good.
Help my words encourage and comfort others.
Amen

51

Observing baptismal anniversaries

Faith Themes

In baptism we enter into new life in Christ.
The sacrament of baptism is filled with action and meaning.

Natural Teachable Moments

- On the anniversary of your child's baptism
- On the anniversary of your own baptism
- As your family prepares to celebrate the baptism of a new member

IT WAS NOT VERY LONG AGO that your child was welcomed into your family. There are the memories of birth, the first days at home, and the gentle expectations surrounding the new life. These memories can be stirred when you run across a birth announcement or photos or videotapes of the event. Not too long ago your child was also initiated into new life in Jesus; she became permanently bonded in Christ through **baptism.** In the process your relationship with your child became deeper than that of parent to child. You and your child became equal members in the family of God, with Christ at the head.

How does your awareness of this deeper bond influence your relationship with your child, now and as she ages?

Starting the Conversation

Place a photo, a candle, or other memorabilia from your child's baptism in the center of the dining table before your next family meal. Share a memory of her baptism that she may not be familiar with. Tell her about why her baptism was an important choice for you.

To Help You Connect

To help your child better appreciate the tradition of faith in your family, you may want to share with her stories of your own baptism. Talk about the choice of your name, your godparents, and baptismal gown. Where was the church, and who came? View photos or a video of the baptism with your child and end with a prayer of thanks for the gift of faith.

TO SUPPORT YOU

SUGGESTED BIBLE READING
Peter calls people to repent and be baptized: Acts 2:1–38

WHAT THE CHURCH SAYS ABOUT THIS TOPIC
Baptism, the first of the seven **sacraments**, frees us from **original sin** and is necessary for salvation. It gives us new life in Jesus Christ through the **Holy Spirit**. Traditionally, there are two methods of baptism: immersion and the pouring on of water. Immersion is the plunging of a person into water. This method was used in Christianity's early days; those desiring to be baptized were immersed in a lake or river. Later, people were baptized in special rooms or buildings, called baptistries, that housed baptismal fonts. Today, baptismal fonts or pools are found in all Catholic churches. Immersion was reintroduced into the Western church after the **Second Vatican Council** and is the preferred form of baptism

for infants and is recommended for adults as well. However, the popular method of baptism in many parishes is still infusion, or the pouring of water over a person's head.

During the rite of baptism, there are gestures, words, and symbols that help make visible the meaning of the sacrament. The person being baptized is immersed in water or has it poured over his or her head. Dressed in white, he or she is signed with the **sign of the cross,** and hears the proclamation of the word of God. Then the initiate (the person being baptized) is anointed with both the **oil of catechumens** and **chrism** (another holy oil, also called "myrrh"), and is also given a candle lit from the Easter candle. The baptismal water symbolizes death and new life; the white garment shows that the person baptized has risen with Christ; the sign of the cross reminds us of the redemption won by Christ for us on the cross; the chrism signifies our receiving the gift of the Holy Spirit; the candle lit from the Easter candle signifies the light of Christ, which is to shine through the life of the newly baptized.

Ordinarily a bishop, priest, or deacon administers a baptism. However, in cases of emergency, such as a life-or-death situation, even someone who is not baptized can baptize another. All that is necessary is to pour water over the person who is receiving the baptism and say: "I baptize you in the name of the Father, and of the Son, and of the Holy Spirit."

A Prayer Moment with Your Child

Let's meet Jesus in prayer, thanking him for making us part of his community:

Loving Jesus, thank you for welcoming me into the church through baptism.

Help me live out my responsibilities as a member of your family.

Amen

52

Living with a sense of awe and mystery

Faith Themes

The Catholic faith contains, and honors, mystery.
St. Thomas Aquinas wrote about the mystery of God's love.

Natural Teachable Moments

- When observing your child's ease in believing
- When your child learns a profound religious truth or engages you in a general discussion about God
- When your child is appreciating the wonders of creation

THOMAS AQUINAS (1225–1274) WAS BORN TO A NOBLE FAMILY IN ITALY. His parents wanted Thomas to become the abbot for a great Benedictine monastery. But Thomas wanted to join a new community dedicated to preaching and teaching: the Dominicans. Since his parents opposed this plan, they imprisoned Thomas in their castle, hoping he would relent. Instead, Thomas ran away to become a Dominican.

A brilliant teacher and theologian, Thomas helped define the **mystery** that is the **real presence** of Jesus Christ in the **Eucharist.** He was also a mystic. Late in his life, while celebrating **Mass,** Thomas had a powerful vision of Jesus. It caused him to cease what had been a career of much-admired spiritual writing. He said the experience made him realize that "all I have written seems like straw" compared to the great mystery of God's love for us.

In 1323, Pope John XXII pronounced Thomas Aquinas a saint. Today St. Thomas Aquinas is considered by many Catholics to be the Church's greatest theologian.

Starting the Conversation

God's infinite love is a mystery that cannot be fully explained, but it can be experienced and celebrated. Share with your child examples of things that you love so dearly that they seem to make life worth living. Invite him to tell you about the people and things he loves. Ask him what special thing he would like to do with you or with the whole family that would be a celebration of love.

To Help You Listen

In conversations with your child, you will often ask for his opinion on a matter of faith or for a suggestion for putting that faith into everyday practice. Keep in mind that there is no one right answer to such a question; there are many right answers! Throughout your discussions, allow your child to voice his feelings freely and to come up with specific family commitments and other ways of living faith in daily life that both you and he are comfortable with. Be careful not to press upon your child specific feelings or actions; this will come across as coercive, and he will likely reject your input, in spirit if not in deed. If you make decisions together, you are more likely to obtain his approval and strengthen the bond between you while respecting his unique spirituality.

TO SUPPORT YOU

SUGGESTED BIBLE READING

In God's great love for us, God will provide for our every need: Matthew 6:25–33

WHAT THE CHURCH SAYS ABOUT THIS TOPIC

Some things in this universe cannot be explained because humanity has yet to learn the answer. Other things cannot be fully explained because these are so "of God" that they cannot be contained in this life by our human minds, let alone be put into words. These things we humbly accept and hold in a respectful sense of mystery. The Catholic Church defines *mystery* as a religious truth that we can know only through God's revelation and that we cannot fully understand. In the Catholic tradition there are many mysteries. For example, the real presence of Jesus in the Eucharist, the incarnation of Jesus as both God and man, and the **Trinity** as three persons in one.

Perhaps the ultimate mystery is, Who or what is God? In some religious faiths, humans are not supposed to even try to explain or name this. Catholicism teaches that God is most completely revealed in the life and teaching of Jesus. In the book of Matthew, Jesus talks about the mystery of the Father's love. He says that this love is so great that God will provide for our every need, if we would just give up fear and live in faith. Jesus tells us to place our dependence on God—where it rightfully lies—instead of on our own efforts, which he compares to independently trying to reap and sow, harvest and store. When we are living in the **kingdom of God,** we need to do none of these things. God knows our needs and how to fill them better than we do. But as we are beings with **free will,** what prohibits God from doing so is our own sinfulness and lack of faith.

A Prayer Moment with Your Child

Let's pray together to our Father, whose love for us is so wonderful
and mysterious that it is beyond our understanding:

God, thank you for your great love,

which is the root of all creation.

It moves the universe and sustains my very life.

Help me always to trust in you.

Amen

Topical Index of Natural Teachable Moments

Holidays

- On Father's Day, when family and community talk involves honoring fathers (#1)

- When preparing for a family trip to a place with foreign cultures and customs (#4)

- Before a May crowning ritual or anytime in May, Mary's month (#5)

- When your family is planning where and how you'll be celebrating religious holidays, such as Easter and Christmas (#6)

- At a holiday meal, party, or feast, when good food and good company are plentiful (#11)

- When making your New Year's resolutions or explaining to your child what these are (#30)

- During your child's birthday party (#36)

- Before an Advent or Christmas family tradition, such as setting out an Advent wreath or decorating the Christmas tree (#44)

- When you and your child watch a Christmas special on TV or video (#44)

Media

- When watching a TV program or cartoon about families or father figures (#1)

- When your child sees the pope or other church figure on TV blessing the crowds (#2)

- When watching a movie or TV show that employs negative stereotypes (#4)

- When you and your child watch a movie, TV show, or news program featuring someone's heroic deeds (#10)

- When your child watches a movie, TV show, or news program about a disturbing example of social injustice (#18)

- After you and your child have heard or watched some particularly bad news in the media (#27)

- On a rainy Sunday afternoon when your child has already spent time in front of the TV, computer, or video games (#32)

- When your child sees informational ads, commercials, or documentaries about famine, wars, environmental neglect, and so on (#34)
- When your child watches a movie, TV show, or news program about a prodigy or person with exceptional abilities (#39)
- When the media covers a story about damage to the environment (#41)

School

- After your child brings home a noticeably good or bad report card (#3)
- On your child's first day of school or with a new club or team (#5)
- A couple of weeks after your child's first day of school or after joining a new club or sports team (#14)
- Before your child's first day at school or camp (#16)
- When your child brings home a report card (#20)
- When your child has trouble with a "teacher's pet" at school or a coach's favorite on a sports team (#21)
- After your child fails a test or gets into trouble at school (#28)
- When your child feels that she is not accepted by the "in" crowd (#31)
- When your child tells you about a social injustice or environmental problem discussed in school (#34)

- When you learn that a school bully or neighborhood gang is harassing your child, and after you have taken any necessary safety precautions or disciplinary action (#35)
- Before a family trip, or when your child is studying different countries and cultures (#49)

Relationships

- When your family is about to have an addition, young or old (#5)
- Before a family reunion, or when visiting grandparents or attending a get-together with extended family (#12)
- When you see your child playing with a new friend in the schoolyard, playground, or neighborhood (#14)
- Before you spend a few hours away from home while someone else stays with your child (#14)
- When going to visit grandparents or when a favorite relative is coming to stay (#17)
- When your child's new friend makes a big impression on her (#17)
- When you tell your child that she will be having a sitter or time with your spouse because you will be out with a friend (#17)
- When your child feels that you or another family member favors a sibling over her, or when you find yourself

making comparisons between your children (#21)

- After your child has a fight with a sibling or other child (#23)
- When your child witnesses you and your spouse or other family members quarreling (#23)
- After you and your spouse decide to reinitiate or repair a broken relationship with a relative or neighbor (#29)
- When your child has teased, injured, fought with, or stolen from a person in the community (#29)
- When your child becomes selfish or unwilling to share with others (#29)
- When your child attends a wedding or a renewal-of-vows ceremony (#30)
- When your child has a crush on someone who will not return her affections (#37)
- When a relative, exchange student, or other person moves in with your family (#45)
- When you have a new neighbor or there's a new child in school (#45)
- When someone in your child's regular group of friends introduces a new person into the circle (#45)
- On the birthday of your child's grandparent (#46)
- After your child has questioned your authority as a parent and why he

should have to follow your orders (#46)

- When your child complains about a sibling being "strange" or acting differently than others (when you know this behavior is simply the sibling's personality) (#49)
- After you or your spouse has just apologized for making a harsh criticism (#50)

Social Concerns

- When your child asks about a stereotype he has encountered (#4)
- After you, your child, or another family member has just made a judgment—or repeated someone else's judgment—based on a stereotype (#4)
- When your family makes plans to do service work together (#18)
- When your child observes or reflects on poor, vulnerable, and unjustly treated people in this world (#26)
- When your child sees others make fun of children or adults who look "different" or himself makes fun of someone different (#28)
- When your child is discriminated against because of personality, abilities, ethnicity, or faith (#31)
- When your parish collects food for a community pantry or a holiday meal (#34)

- When you observe your child exhibiting a prejudice, especially the subtle kind revealed in casual speech (#38)
- When your child is the subject of, or contributes to, discrimination (#38)
- When your child witnesses you or your spouse being prejudicial toward a person or group of people (#38)
- When your family recycles household materials (#41)
- When your child is with you in a grocery store where you are buying "green" products (#41)
- On Earth Day or around school events that show care for the environment (#41)
- When someone in your family does volunteer work (#42)
- When your child shows clear concern for a societal problem or a person who is in need (#42)
- When political oppression, social injustice, or genocide create a refugee crisis (#47)
- When a family of a different ethnic group from yours moves into the neighborhood (#49)

Church and Faith

- When your child sees you or someone else, such as a sports figure, make the sign of the cross (#2)
- When you first suggest that you and your child try praying together, if you do not already have regular prayer time (#6)
- When your child wonders how she, or the world, began (#7)
- When your child is feeling unsure about whether God loves her (#11)
- During Ordinary Time in the church liturgical year (#22)
- On the way home from Sunday Mass (#24)
- When your child asks "Why is . . . ?" or "Why does . . . ?" about the world (#27)
- When your child fears that the world may really be just a bad or ugly place (#27)
- When your child is preparing to receive a sacrament (#30)
- When your child interrupts your personal prayer or quiet reflection time (#33)
- During a Friday or Saturday family meal in preparation for Sunday Mass (#36)
- When one of your children is preparing for first communion (#36)
- Before your family goes to Mass together on Sunday to start the week (#48)
- On the anniversary of your child's baptism (#51)

- On the anniversary of your own baptism (#51)
- As the family prepares to celebrate the baptism of a new member (#51)
- When observing your child's ease in believing (#52)
- When your child learns a profound religious truth or engages you in a general discussion about God (#52)

Morality and Character

- When your child worries about "bad" people or questions the nature of things (#7)
- After your child uses the slang expression, "'s all good." (#7)
- When your child is being willful and threatens you with bad behavior (#8)
- When your child is reluctant to act on your authority alone or challenges the authority of an adult who responds, "Because I told you to." (#8)
- After you, your child, or another family member has made a decision that results in clearly observable consequences (#8)
- As your child plans to go to a sports event, concert, or convention featuring one of his pop idols (#10)
- When your child has done something wrong and doesn't seem to care (#19)
- When your child has been teased by neighbors, friends, or family (#20)

- When your child is becoming overly competitive (#21)
- When someone your child knows is making bad decisions and courting trouble (#26)
- When you and your child witness road rage (#28)
- When another child or team is being overly competitive about a sporting event or regularly played game, such as a neighborhood baseball game or a video game (#35)
- When your child is teased, excluded, or lied to (#35)
- When an internal trait or mark of character in your child stands out (#39)
- When your child observes or experiences a little act of kindness (#40)
- When your child does something good and kind (#43)
- When your child helps without being asked (#43)
- When you child is gentle and forgiving (#43)
- When your child sees another child misbehaving in public (#46)
- When your child has damaged property in the house, whether intentionally, through horseplay, or by accident (#50)

Changes and Challenges

- During times of difficulty or when big decisions must be made, when the family comes together in prayer or discussion (#6)

- As the family is preparing to relocate or when a good friend moves away (#9)

- When your child's summer plans fall through or she must attend summer school or another academic program (#9)

- When your family makes a household change, such as tightening the budget or putting limits on TV watching and Internet surfing (#9)

- When you or your spouse is going back to work after being an at-home parent (#13)

- When your family loses or gains a member in your home—whether young or old, human or animal (#13)

- When an older sibling goes off to college or moves away from home (#13)

- After your child or a sibling is lost and then found (#16)

- When you, your spouse, or another significant adult in your child's life changes jobs to do something more in line with a calling to ministry (#18)

- When your child struggles to believe in God (#19)

- When a tragedy occurs in your child's world and she views God or the world with suspicion or fear (#19)

- When someone your child knows is gravely ill and is visited by a priest to be given last rites (#23)

- When someone your child knows is sick, has just received bad news about his or her health, or is experiencing misfortune (#26)

- Before or after your family relocates (#31)

- When your child or someone she loves gets sick or is stricken with a serious illness (#37)

- When your child begins to learn about death (#37)

- After the sudden death of a friend or family member (#47)

- When a natural disaster strikes a community or another country, leaving pain, destruction, famine, disease, orphans, or homeless (#47)

- When a family member is experiencing burnout at work or school (#48)

- When someone in the family is very sick (or dying) (#48)

Family Routines

- During ordinary family time, such as a meal, a weekend outing, or a game (#1)

- Whenever you wish to bless your child, such as when he leaves on a school trip or for an overnight with a friend (#2)
- While driving your child to or from an athletic or artistic practice (#3)
- When your child shows interest in a hobby or discipline (#3)
- When your child sees firefighters, police officers, soldiers, or any public servant on TV, in malls, in parades, or on the street (#10)
- When your child is admiring the natural wonders of our world (#11)
- When celebrating a family tradition that your child loves (#12)
- When looking at our country's flag or that of another country (#12)
- During family meals or when planning for the upcoming weekend (#15)
- While driving your child to and from activities (#15)
- When tucking your child into bed at night (#15, #33)
- When you and your child are on your way to a large shopping center, amusement park, or other crowded area (#16)
- When you are teaching your child a new skill or activity (#20)
- When you and your child find some mundane thing suddenly amusing or entertaining (#22)
- When you and your child walk the dog, water flowers, visit a neighbor, cook, or perform another ordinary task (#22)
- During a family dinner (#24)
- When your child expresses enjoyment of a family activity or some past family event (#24)
- When your family is choosing the name for a new pet (#25)
- When your child makes a friend with an uncommon name (#25)
- When your child asks what your or another family member's middle name is or why (#25)
- After teaching your child how to cook a particular dish that you gather to eat together (#32)
- When putting together a family album or collage (#32)
- When you walk with your child: accompanying her to school, strolling through the neighborhood after a meal, or hiking through a park or along a beach (#33)
- When your child enjoys, and excels in, a subject, hobby, or sport (#39)
- When planting flowers, shrubs, or a garden with your child (#40)

- When your child measures his increasing height over time (#40)
- When your family is discussing the occupational choices of friends, neighbors, parishioners, or other members of society (#42)
- When you share the story of your child's birth (#44)
- During the family meal (#50)
- When your child is appreciating the wonders of creation (#52)

Guide to Scripture Readings

The Life and Teachings of Jesus Christ

- Jesus shows us how to *be* through the Beatitudes: **Matthew 5:1–10** (#43)

- Jesus explains the Ten Commandments and teaches us about loving our enemies: **Matthew 5:17–48** (#35)

- In God's great love for us, God will provide for our every need: **Matthew 6:25–33** (#52)

- The kingdom of God is compared to the tiny mustard seed that grows to be the largest of plants: **Matthew 13:31–32** (#40)

- Jesus renames Peter and gives him authority to head the Church: **Matthew 16:18–19** (#25)

- Jesus teaches us the Great Commandment: **Matthew 22:37–38** (#42)

- Jesus' parable of the Last Judgment tells us that we will be judged according to our faith and how we treat others: **Matthew 25:31–46** (#47)

- Jesus tells us he will be with us always: **Matthew 28:20** (#22)

- Jesus' birth is announced to Mary, who in a spirit of humility praises God for choosing her: **Luke 1:26–38 and 46–50** (#5)

- The story of Christ's birth and Mary's reflection on these events: **Luke 2:4–14 and 19–20** (#44)

- Simeon meets the holy family in the temple of Jerusalem: **Luke 2:25–32** (#4)

- Mary and Joseph search for and find Jesus, who grows up obedient to his parents: **Luke 2:41–51** (#46)

- Jesus calls Peter to follow him, and Peter answers the call: **Luke 5:1–11** (#39)

- Jesus sends forth his disciples to heal: **Luke 9:1–6** (#23)

- Jesus teaches about mercy and love by telling a parable: **Luke 10:25–37** (#38)

- Jesus tells the parable of the prodigal son and the forgiving father: **Luke 15:11–24** (#28)

- Jesus tells the Pharisees that the kingdom of God is already here: **Luke 17:21** (#17)

- Jesus associates with and forgives a public sinner: **Luke 19:2–9** (#29)

- Jesus promises salvation to a criminal who was being crucified with him: **Luke 23:39–43** (#37)

- Jesus walks and dines with two disciples on the road to Emmaus: **Luke 24:13–35** (#45)

- The work of the Spirit is like a wind that blows where it chooses: **John 3:8** (#9)

- Listening to God leads us to Jesus: **John 6:45** (#33)

- Jesus tells us he is the bread of life: **John 6:47–58** (#48)

- Jesus speaks of the relationship between himself and the Father and us: **John 14:23** (#1)

- Jesus tells us we are friends when we follow him and do God's will: **John 15:14** (#14)

- Jesus empowers the disciples with the Holy Spirit to continue his mission: **John 20:19–22** (#20)

- An account of Jesus and the disciples celebrating the Last Supper: **1 Corinthians 11:23–26** (#24)

Lessons and Heroes from the Old Testament

- God creates the world and people: **Genesis 1:1–2:4 and Genesis 2:4–25** (#7)

- God gives creation to humans, and creation rejoices: **Genesis 1:28–31 and Psalm 96:11–13** (#41)

- God creates heaven and earth and people: **Genesis 1:1–31** (#27)

- God provides food for the man and woman he created: **Genesis 1:29** (#11)

- Adam and Eve sin, and humanity falls from grace: **Genesis 3:1–24** (#19)

- Abraham is put to the test: **Genesis 22:1–13** (#3)

- Jacob deceives his brother: **Genesis 25:19–34; 27:1–45** (#21)

- God delivers the Ten Commandments through Moses: **Exodus 20:1–17** (#30)

- Moses urges the Israelites to take the commandments to heart and to teach their children: **Deuteronomy 6:4–9** (#10)

- Two stories show us two moral choices: **Ruth 1–4 and 2 Samuel 11:1–17** (#8)

- God comforts the Jews in exile: **Isaiah 40:1–2** (#31)

Lessons and Stories of the New Testament Church

- The institution of the Eucharist at the Last Supper is remembered: **Luke 22:14–20** (#32)

- Peter calls people to repent and be baptized: **Acts 2:1–38** (#51)

- Peter speaks of baptism in Spirit and following Jesus: **Acts 2:38** (#13)

- The early Christians demonstrate deep love for God and for one another: **Acts 2:42–47** (#36)

- An account of Jesus and the disciples celebrating the Last Supper: **1 Corinthians 11:23–26** (#24)

- Through the Holy Spirit, we are one body with many parts: **1 Corinthians 12:12–21** (#49)

- The fruits of the Holy Spirit are listed: **Galatians 5:22–23** (#18)

- All are asked to bear one another's burdens: **Galatians 6:2** (#16)

- As the people of God, we are like stones in a holy structure, held together by Christ: **Ephesians 2:19–22** (#15)

- The church has holy characteristics: **Ephesians 4:1–6, 15–16** (#12)

- Paul writes a letter of joy and prays unceasingly for the early Christian community: **Philippians 1:1–11** (#26)

- James cautions us to regulate our speech: **James 3:1–12** (#50)

- The early Christian community is urged to turn from evil and do good: **1 Peter 3:8–12** (#6)

- Everyone who loves is of God and knows God: **1 John 4:7** (#34)

- Through love, God lives in us and we live in God: **1 John 4:7–12** (#2)

Index of Faith Themes by Category

These five categories—**God, Jesus, The Church, Worship,** and **Morality**—are the basic categories used for instruction in the Catechism of the Catholic Church. The number in parentheses after each item indicates the lesson in which that Faith Theme appears.

God

God is loving Father to us, as taught by Jesus. (#1)

We are children of God and can therefore have an intimate father-child relationship with God. (#1)

The love of the Father, Son, and Holy Spirit is the source of all love. (#2)

We use the sign of the cross as a prayer of blessing. (#2)

God wants our faith, not sacrifice. (#3)

Abraham's near sacrifice is a great lesson for us. (#3)

Simeon in the Bible was able to recognize who Jesus was because he listened to the Holy Spirit. (#4)

We can, with the Spirit's help, learn to see people for who they are. (#4)

The human family is created in the image and likeness of God. (#7)

God created everything good, and there are good aspects of things we usually think of as bad. (#7)

God created us because God loves us. (#11)

God gives us what we need and only wants the best for us. (#11)

Adam and Eve's distrust of God had definite effects on the human condition. (#19)

God promised to send us a savior, Jesus Christ. (#19)

God is present in everyday life and invites us to be in his presence. (#22)

God says that the world is good. (#27)

God created everything out of love for us; all of creation is good. (#27)

St. Thomas Aquinas wrote about the mystery of God's love. (#52)

Jesus Christ

The Holy Spirit is like the wind, which blows where it wills. (#9)

We grow in the gifts of the Holy Spirit. (#9)

Our heroes help form our conscience. (#10)

Free will leads to moral responsibility. (#10)

Jesus is the model of love and goodness for our lives. (#22)

We can reach out to others who are suffering. (#37)

Jesus redeemed us from our sins through his life, death, and resurrection. (#37)

Jesus sees possibilities in Peter, and in all of us. (#39)

Jesus invites his followers to enter the kingdom of God. (#39)

Small acts of kindness and love yield a great harvest. (#40)

The parable of the mustard seed teaches us about the kingdom of God. (#40)

The Beatitudes describe the Christian way to live. (#43)

Jesus shows us how we can be truly happy and share happiness with others. (#43)

Jesus' birth teaches us about humility and finding God in unexpected places. (#44)

The church recognizes corporal and spiritual works of mercy. (#47)

The Church

Mary said yes to God in faith and trust, and she became the mother of Jesus. (#5)

Mary loves and prays for us. (#5)

Through the Holy Spirit, Christ unifies us and makes us holy. (#12)

The marks of Christ's Church are one, holy, catholic, and apostolic. (#12)

We all need companions on our faith journey. (#14)

Jesus gives us the church as our community of spiritual friends and companions so that we can help one another and serve God's kingdom. (#14)

The family's love for one another is a reflection of the enduring love between Christ and his people. (#15)

The family is also known as the "domestic church." (#15)

Jesus works through us to reach all people. (#17)

Jesus is with us through love and in a special way through the sacraments. (#17)

St. Katharine Drexel followed the Spirit. (#18)

When we work with God we receive the fruits of the Holy Spirit. (#18)

Every child is special. (#21)

A Christian family's solidarity mirrors the solidarity of Christ's church. (#21)

A person's name has spiritual importance. (#25)

Jesus renamed Peter and gave us leaders in the church. (#25)

It is our privilege and responsibility to pray for our children. (#26)

St. Monica gave us an example of faithfulness in prayer. (#26)

Jesus' community is the church. (#36)

Jesus calls us to share his love with others. (#36)

Being one in Christ enables unity in diversity. (#49)

The church is one, expressed in many ways. (#49)

The Catholic faith contains, and honors, mystery. (#52)

Worship

We can have new life in God. (#13)

The sacraments of initiation help us with transition. (#13)

The Holy Spirit helps us feel loved. (#20)

The Holy Spirit is God's active presence among us. (#20)

God forgives us and heals our bodies and our souls. (#23)

The two sacraments of healing are penance and anointing of the sick. (#23)

Going to Mass and honoring the Sabbath help unite families. (#24)

The celebration of the Eucharist is the center of parish life. (#24)

God loves each person infinitely, eternally, and without condition. (#28)

We reflect God's love in our relationships with one another when we love unconditionally and forgive one another. (#28)

Jesus forgave Zacchaeus and dined with him. (#29)

By celebrating the sacrament of penance, we are reconciled with God and others. (#29)

God is with his people, even in exile. (#31)

God gives comfort and hope to those who are outcast and who suffer. (#31)

In celebrating the Mass, we remember what Jesus has done for us. (#32)

At the Last Supper, Jesus gave us a way to remember him. (#32)

Prayer is a relationship with God, and there are many different ways to pray. (#33)

When we pray, we are listening to and talking with God. (#33)

We can welcome Jesus into our lives. (#45)

How two disciples welcomed Jesus. (#45)

For Catholics, the Eucharist is the real presence of Christ. (#48)

Jesus' presence in the Mass and the Eucharist feeds our souls. (#48)

In Baptism we enter into new life in Christ. (#51)

The sacrament of baptism is filled with action and meaning. (#51)

Morality

Our life priorities are moral choices. (#6)

God wants us to respect others and live in peace. (#6)

God gives us the freedom to make our own choices. (#8)

Moral choices affect our relationships with God and other people; moral decisions have moral consequences. (#8)

The Holy Spirit guides our choices to help us live in peace. (#16)

Jesus teaches us to love, respect, and care for one another. (#16)

God is committed to us and wants our commitment. (#30)

Using the Ten Commandments to guide our actions, we make good moral decisions and stay faithful to God. (#30)

All life is sacred. (#34)

Small acts of social justice make a big difference. (#34)

Jesus challenges us to love our enemies. (#35)

The fourth through tenth commandments teach us how to live in right relationship with others. (#35)

All people are children of God. (#38)

Through his words and deeds, Jesus showed us how to love others. (#38)

Gospel of Life refers to an important document in the Catholic Church. (#41)

All life is a sacred gift from God, and as God's people we have a special responsibility to care for the environment. (#41)

We are to love as God loves. (#42)

Each one of us is called to be holy. (#42)

God has given our parents to us, and we are called to honor and obey them. (#46)

Jesus obeyed his parents. (#46)

Jesus calls us to eternal life with our Father in heaven. (#47)

A moral life commits us to truth in our words and deeds. (#50)

Jesus helps us act responsibly toward others and with respect. (#50)

Index of Proper Names and Important Terms

Additional Resources

Further Reading

These fine books are available at the publisher's website, such as LoyolaBooks.org, at Amazon.com, BarnesandNoble.com, or at your favorite local or online bookstore.

Chesto, Kathleen O'Connell. *Family Prayer for Family Times: Traditions, Celebrations, and Rituals.* Mystic, CT: Twenty-Third Publications, 1995.

_____. *Raising Kids Who Care: About Themselves, About Their World, About Each Other.* Liguori, MO: Liguori Lifespan, 2003.

Coloroso, Barbara. *Kids Are Worth It: Giving Your Child the Gift of Inner Discipline.* New York: Quill, 2002.

Damon, William. *The Moral Child: Nurturing Children's Natural Moral Growth.* New York: The Free Press, 1990.

Giannetti, Charlene C., and Margaret Sagarese. *Good Parents, Tough Times: How Your Catholic Faith Provides Hope and Guidance in Times of Crisis.* Chicago: Loyola Press, 2005.

Leonard, Richard. *Movies That Matter: Reading Film through the Lens of Faith.* Chicago: Loyola Press, 2006.

McGrath, Tom. *Raising Faith-Filled Kids: Ordinary Opportunities to Nurture Spirituality at Home.* Chicago: Loyola Press, 2000.

O'Connell-Cahill, Catherine. *moms@myspiritualgrowth.com: Meditations and Cool Websites for Active Moms.* Chicago: ACTA Publications.

Odell, Catherine, and Margaret Savitskas. *Loyola Kids Book of Everyday Prayers.* Chicago: Loyola Press, 2002.

Parisi, Al, and Ann Marie Parisi. *Lunch Bag Notes: Everyday Advice from a Dad to His Daughter.* Chicago: Loyola Press, 2004.

Parisi, Al, and Anthony Parisi. *More Lunch Bag Notes: Everyday Advice from a Dad to His Son.* Chicago: Loyola Press, 2005.

Roy, Denise. *My Monastery Is a Minivan: Where the Daily Is Divine and Routine Becomes Prayer.* Chicago: Loyola Press, 2001.

Viets, Amy. *Making Faith Fun: 132 Spiritual Activities You Can Do with Your Kids.* Skokie, IL: ACTA Publications, 2006.

Vogt, Susan V. *Raising Kids Who Will Make a Difference: Helping Your Family Live with Integrity, Value Simplicity, and Care for Others.* Chicago: Loyola Press, 2002.

Welborn, Amy. *Loyola Kids Book of Heroes: Stories of Catholic Heroes and Saints throughout History.* Chicago: Loyola Press, 2003.

Wright, Wendy M. *Sacred Dwelling: A Spirituality of Family Life.* Leavenworth, KS: Forest of Peace Publishing, 1994.

Websites

In addition to the sites listed below, most Catholic dioceses and archdioceses have an office for family life ministries; check in your local area.

www.familyministries.org
The Archdiocese of Chicago's Family Ministries site

www.findinggod.org
Award-winning site offering online faith formation, articles, activities, prayers, and other resources serving religious educators and parents alike; sponsored by Loyola Press

www.flrl.org
The Archdiocese of New York's Family Life and Respect Life site

www.homefaith.com
Award-winning site offering spiritual help for families and a depth of practical resources; from Claretian Publications

www.ipj-ppj.org/PPJN--2dNEW.htm
"Parenting for Peace and Justice Network"— an interfaith, interracial, transnational association offering workshops, newsletters, greeting cards, gifts, and other resources for families that promote well-being, peace, and justice; from the Institute for Peace and Justice, Kathy and Jim McGinnis, coordinators

www.susanvogt.net
"Family Matters"—articles, resources, and activities on marriage, parenting, and spirituality, plus more than 150 archived Marriage Moments and Parenting Pointers for leaders to use in newsletters, bulletins, and on websites; from author Susan Vogt

Newsletters

These fine newsletters can be obtained by contacting the publisher. In addition to those listed below, many Catholic diocesan and archdiocesan offices have newsletters for families; check in your local area.

At Home with Our Faith; Claretian Publications

Finding God Parent Newsletter; Loyola Press

A Special Invitation

Loyola Press invites you to become one of our Loyola Press Advisors! Join our unique online community of people willing to share with us their thoughts and ideas about Catholic life and faith. By sharing your perspective, you will help us improve our books and serve the greater Catholic community.

From time to time, registered advisors are invited to participate in online surveys and discussion groups. Most surveys will take less than ten minutes to complete. Loyola Press will recognize your time and efforts with gift certificates and prizes. Your personal information will be held in strict confidence. Your participation will be for research purposes only, and at no time will we try to sell you anything.

Please consider this opportunity to help Loyola Press improve our products and better serve you and the Catholic community. To learn more or to join, visit **www.SpiritedTalk.org** and register today.

—THE LOYOLA PRESS ADVISORY TEAM